About This Book

Why is this topic important?

In stark contrast to most sales books published today, this book is organized around many ideas that haven't been applied to professional selling before. You will not find a repackaged version of yester-year's sales philosophy or the "do it like me" testimonials of successful salespeople who were in environments that are completely different than your own. The applicability of such content is at best limited and at worst expired. Instead, we are bringing you legitimately new selling principles that have consistently driven sales success in today's reality.

What can you achieve with this book?

Sales Chaos is the first book to apply the scientific principles of chaos theory and complex systems to the sales profession so that you can have better sales conversations with your customers. It is written to provide a no-holds-barred explanation of what professional selling has become and to help you learn how to identify patterns you can use to overcome the challenges you are facing in this new reality. No matter whether you are new to sales or a seasoned professional, *Sales Chaos* provides the key information an individual seller should know to turn scientific theory into sales results.

How is this book organized?

The book is divided into core themes for learning a new approach to professional selling:

Section 1: Thinking Differently
- Chapter 1: Chaos Reigns
- Chapter 2: Fundamentals of Sales Chaos: Butterflies
- Chapter 3: Fundamentals of Sales Chaos: Anchor Points

To help you accelerate your understanding of these two themes, the end of each chapter also provides worksheets, tools, and self-assessments to help you build on your own current knowledge and skills.

About Pfeiffer

Pfeiffer serves the professional development and hands-on resource needs of training and human resource practitioners and gives them products to do their jobs better. We deliver proven ideas and solutions from experts in HR development and HR management, and we offer effective and customizable tools to improve workplace performance. From novice to seasoned professional, Pfeiffer is the source you can trust to make yourself and your organization more successful.

Essential Knowledge Pfeiffer produces insightful, practical, and comprehensive materials on topics that matter the most to training and HR professionals. Our Essential Knowledge resources translate the expertise of seasoned professionals into practical, how-to guidance on critical workplace issues and problems. These resources are supported by case studies, worksheets, and job aids and are frequently supplemented with CD-ROMs, websites, and other means of making the content easier to read, understand, and use.

Essential Tools Pfeiffer's Essential Tools resources save time and expense by offering proven, ready-to-use materials—including exercises, activities, games, instruments, and assessments—for use during a training or team-learning event. These resources are frequently offered in looseleaf or CD-ROM format to facilitate copying and customization of the material.

Pfeiffer also recognizes the remarkable power of new technologies in expanding the reach and effectiveness of training. While e-hype has often created whizbang solutions in search of a problem, we are dedicated to bringing convenience and enhancements to proven training solutions. All our e-tools comply with rigorous functionality standards. The most appropriate technology wrapped around essential content yields the perfect solution for today's on-the-go trainers and human resource professionals.

www.pfeiffer.com

Essential resources for training and HR professionals

About the American Society for Training & Development

The American Society for Training & Development (ASTD) is the world's largest professional association dedicated to the training and development field. In more than one hundred countries, ASTD's members work in organizations of all sizes, in the private and public sectors, as independent consultants, and as suppliers. Members connect locally in 130 U.S. chapters and with thirty international partners.

ASTD started in 1943 and in recent years has widened the profession's focus to align learning and performance to organizational results and is a sought-after voice on critical public policy issues. For more information, visit www.astd.org.

Join Us at
Pfeiffer.com
▼

Pfeiffer®
An Imprint of
WILEY

Register at **www.pfeiffer.com/email**
for more information on our publications,
authors, and to receive special offers.

SALES CHAOS

Using Agility Selling to Think and Sell Differently

TIM OHAI
BRIAN LAMBERT

Pfeiffer

A Wiley Imprint
www.pfeiffer.com

Published by Pfeiffer
An Imprint of Wiley
989 Market Street, San Francisco, CA 94103-1741
www.pfeiffer.com

For additional copies/bulk purchases of this book in the U.S. please contact
800-274-4434.

Pfeiffer books and products are available through most bookstores. To contact Pfeiffer
directly call our Customer Care Department within the U.S. at 800-274-4434, outside
the U.S. at 317-572-3985, fax 317-572-4002, or visit www.pfeiffer.com.

Library of Congress Cataloging-in-Publication Data

Ohai, Tim, 1971-
  Sales chaos : using agility selling to think and sell differently / Tim Ohai,
Brian Lambert.
        p. cm.
  Includes bibliographical references and index.
  ISBN 978-0-470-88601-4 (pbk.); 978-1-118-06427-6 (ebk);
978-1-118-06428-3 (ebk); 978-1-118-06429-0 (ebk)
  1. Selling. 2. Chaotic behavior in systems. I. Lambert, Brian. II. Title.
  HF5438.25.O36 2011
  658.85—dc22

                                                    2011008888

Pfeiffer also publishes its books in a variety of electronic formats. Some content that
appears in print may not be available in electronic books.

Acquiring Editor: Matthew Davis   Director of Development: Kathleen Dolan Davies
Production Editor: Michael Kay   Manufacturing Supervisor: Becky Morgan
Editorial Assistant: Michael Zelenko   Graphics: Kulana Grafix
Editor: Rebecca Taff

Printed in the United States of America

Printing   10 9 8 7 6 5 4 3 2 1

Contents

Preface

This section is for those of you who are curious about the science behind our theories. If you just want to learn how to think and sell differently, run ahead to Chapter 1. Obviously, this book is about chaos. Or more specifically, how to harness it. And that will require agility. We haven't run into a senior executive yet who hasn't agreed that agility is important in business. Agility just sounds good, doesn't it? It implies speed, adaptation, decisiveness, alignment, and readiness, even when things are chaotic. But to become agile, you have to understand that agility is more than just a business philosophy or a selling strategy.

AGILITY MEANS INCREASED RESPONSIBILITY FOR THE SALESPERSON

Buyers are demanding more. Higher expectations for attaining business results are being placed on sales professionals by buyers who are expected to make the correct purchase decision. As buyers push for increased cost savings with more scrutiny on spending, procurement functions are growing in scope and scale and will play an expanded role in the buying process moving forward. As a result, salespeople are under increased pressure to attain the goals of both the selling organization and the buying organization. This translates into the need for salespeople to not only accept initial responsibility for the goals, but to maintain that responsibility to ensure the success of both buyer and seller, as defined by each side. The agility selling methodology makes it possible for sales professionals to embrace this responsibility.

AGILITY MEANS INCREASED EMPHASIS ON CONSULTATIVE SELLING

Unfortunately, executive buyers don't believe salespeople really understand their business. To be blunt about it, salespeople need to do a better job in transitioning from product-pushers to problem-solvers. And this requires a true partnership mentality. In response, some salespeople are focusing on developing deeper relationships and personal networks inside their target companies as well within the specific industry. Sales leaders must begin to take more steps to ensure that customers are getting value, not just product.

To differentiate themselves, many sellers have focused on listening, analyzing, problem solving, and questioning to help buyers navigate the complexity of the solution and the plethora of available information. Communication skills such as active listening can help sellers identify root problems and hidden obstacles that affect the buyer's business success. Building rapport, demonstrating patience, and exercising astute timing contribute to building the foundation for a trusting buyer–seller relationship. These higher-level skills are included in the Agility Selling methodology and re-cast the role of learning to the point where learning is mandatory for success.

AGILITY MEANS FASTER AND MORE EFFECTIVE SELLER RESPONSIVENESS

In today's competitive landscape, sales teams must focus on maintaining professionalism with buyers who may not have the same timeframe in mind or who may have strong negotiating skills. Often, these buyers do not even operate within a linear definition of process. This is especially important since buyer decision-making is becoming increasingly more collaborative. Today's seller must stay focused on communicating value to the buyer based on mutually agreed-on goals and objectives, regardless of the state of the interaction process. This requires taking the client's best interest into account while providing a relevant solution to the business issues at hand. Executives don't want to participate in a meeting with irrelevant goals or no clear purpose. The higher the level of the executive, the more customized the message needs to be to resonate, taxing traditional create-once-publish-many-times marketing techniques. The ability to gain access to decision-makers and also have the right conversation is a result of appropriately following the Agility Selling methodology.

AGILITY INCREASES EMPHASIS ON PROFITABILITY

Many sales managers are compensated on gross margin or profitability as well as top-line revenue. This coincides with more firms examining the profitability and productivity of salesperson activity, rather than frequency or volume. As a result, organizations are working hard to ensure their sales team members use time appropriately and productively. Whatever qualifications and experience you possess, the issues you face can best be defined as: becoming a more effective and efficient trusted advisor who can communicate and demonstrate value at every customer interaction. If this is the challenge you seek to address, it can be addressed with the concepts found within Agility Selling.

LOOK FOR THESE ICONS

We have tried to make it easy for you to understand and apply lessons from this book. The following icons used throughout the book will help you zoom in on key points.

Pay Attention!

This icon indicates callouts for our key points from the text that you don't want to overlook. Fail to grasp these key points, and you run the risk of being less effective than you would probably like to be. Make sure you take note of each of these comments, and refer to them frequently. The more you study them, the more you will realize they apply to many situations.

Consider This

This icon indicates comments and extra thinking that cuts to the chase. They point out condensed important concepts and assumptions that form the foundation for harnessing the chaotic randomness around you. You can revisit these ideas to further your thinking in order to continuously improve.

Mirror Moment

This icon indicates you have an opportunity to "look in the mirror". By stopping and reflecting on the content, you are able to take stock of important concepts and determine how your own abilities can be stretched.

Building on the Foundation

This icon indicates ancillary information about the topics covered in the chapter. This icon also provides key definitions of important people who contributed these concepts to professional selling.

Making It Stick

This icon indicates actionable worksheets, job aids, and tools. These are helpful tips and bonus tools found at the end of every key chapter. These help reinforce the important concepts, knowledge, and techniques found in the chapter. They are presented in a way that helps you sell with agility.

Here's to butterflies, anchor points, and snowflakes—and here's to the ability to harness them.

Tim Ohai
Brian Lambert

Acknowledgments

When you sit down to write a book, you know it will be a lot of work. But you never truly appreciate how much work it will be, nor how much you will rely on the help of others. We would like to thank a few of them now.

From Tim:

I have to start with my wife and family. Diana, words cannot begin to express my gratitude for your encouragement, support, and all those pots of coffee I drank by myself. Connor and Caelan, you don't know how helpful those Nintendo breaks were.

While the list of salespeople I have worked with over the years is massive, I must single out two people. Jim Hayes, my first sales manager. Who would've thought the new kid would eventually figure things out, eh? You did. Thank you. And Owen McManamon. What can I say? It's not often people get to work with company presidents who live and breathe professional selling. I cannot say enough how much your friendship both shaped my philosophy and inspired me to step out on my own. Thank you.

From Brian:

I, too, have to start with my wife and family. Donna, thanks for supporting me and always being there. Thanks also for your understanding of the long hours and constant, sales-related conversations. I am sure you still don't have a clue what we wrote about, and that's ok. Thanks to Caitlin, Maleah, and Matthew for helping me take a break and have some fun amidst all the chaos in my job and at home. Thanks to my mom, who taught me the importance of books and knowledge, and to my dad, the consummate sales professional.

From both of us:

While we were constantly bouncing our theory off of other people, we must specifically point out Steve Thompson and Tim Caito, two genuine experts in the world of professional selling. You guys took our idea of agile conversations and gave them the structure they needed in the form of fifteen questions.

We also want to acknowledge the growing number of people who treat sales as a science and not just an art, such as Eric Kerkhoff, Tony Cross, Marcel Brunel, and Scott Barghaan. Let's keep moving the profession of sales forward.

Finally, we would also like to thank the staff of ASTD and Pfeiffer. Professionals like Dean Smith and Matt Davis, who did an amazing job of getting this project off the ground and keeping it from crashing back down to earth.

SECTION
1

Thinking Differently

CHAPTER

1

Chaos Reigns

"Chaos results when the world changes faster than people."

Anonymous

INTRODUCTION

Daniel was driving home from work. It was 8:30 p.m. He was tired, and he knew he would have to get up early tomorrow to get ready for the big sales call with his newest major prospect. As he drove home, his mind slowly recapped the day in an attempt to identify and finalize the growing list of "to-dos" for the coming days. This morning it was up early for a quick workout, then an even quicker breakfast. Within an hour, he had skimmed the daily newspaper as well as four major news websites while simultaneously getting dressed for the day. He had also read two earnings call transcripts from his biggest clients and accomplished a quick scan of his smart phone to determine whether any fires had popped up within his customer base overnight. Luckily for him, things were mostly under control—just an email from his boss asking for an update on three of his opportunities before 2:00 p.m. today (some sort of meeting prep with the Sales VP, he assumed). A quick review of his daily calendar and he was out the door.

The day unfolded around three big sales meetings (sales calls) that he ran today. Two were with prospects, and one

3

meeting was with a client he'd had for about a year. The three meetings were with various levels of decision-makers (some higher in their organization with decision-making power and some lower in their organization but who held considerable influence on others in the organization). None of the meetings today were with a single person. As usual, there were as many as seven people and as few as two people in these meetings. Of course, he was able to talk about the benefits and value of all his 100+ products and fifteen services during his meetings. He was able to discuss pricing options while negotiating price in one of those meetings. "I think I did pretty well on that," he thought to himself. In each of his three calls, the competition was brought up, and he was able to explain his organization's unique value proposition in a way that bashed the competition, but still made a strong case for his company's solution.

Still driving home from work, Daniel took a mental tally and reviewed each of the sales meetings, in an attempt to mentally debrief how well he had done and identify any areas for clarification or possible questions from the people he had met with. During the day, he had managed to arrive on time to all his appointments and keep his energy level up. Now, looking at his face in the rearview mirror, he realized that exhaustion was finally taking over. "At least the day is almost over," he thought.

When he pulled into the driveway it was 9:05 p.m. Looking at his briefcase in the car seat next to him, he instinctively knew what he needed to do. He pulled out his notebook and reviewed the day's notes and made a list of follow-up actions that were highly urgent and another list of actions that could come later. He pulled out a couple of brochures that he had carried with him today. "I never hand these things out," he thought, but he put them right back in their usual briefcase pocket.

He opened up his daily calendar to the day's date and reviewed his notes from the phone calls he had made between his three sales meetings. Daniel quickly highlighted the internal communications and coordination he needed to accomplish in the coming hours in order to keep momentum up with his sales opportunities. "A pretty productive day, but again no sales were closed," he sighed. He finally got out of his car and went inside.

A brief glance at the clock showed it was now 9:15 p.m. He quickly flipped forward in his calendar to skim the remaining three days of the week. The next couple of days had three sales calls each, and then there was Friday. Friday was the quarterly planning meeting at the regional office that began with what Daniel called the "dog and pony show"—individual sales pipeline reviews with the entire team as the audience. "At some point, I have to prepare my whole portfolio of customers and update my spreadsheets . . . and finish my account plans," he thought wearily. "But at least I have a few more days to do it. And besides, as the number one person this quarter, they'll probably cut me some slack."

Sounds familiar, doesn't it? If you are anything like Daniel, the world of professional selling is a constantly moving one. One that requires you to work many long hours for the kind of success that comes far too infrequently. But even when you look at Daniel's story, he is still experiencing success (at least for this quarter). Can you tell why? More specifically, could you do the same thing?

TAKING INVENTORY

Defining what it takes to be successful in sales is arguably the most difficult part of the job. Considering how visible sales results are, any and all missteps can be immediately obvious. And if you are the one experiencing the missteps, the list of excuses for the poor performance can be as long as your arm.

Pause. Let's try an exercise. Picture yourself falling behind in your sales performance. What is causing this current situation? Is it just your personality that is getting in the way? Probably not. Is it some knowledge that you are missing? Perhaps. Is it a set of skills that have slowly lost their value over time? Could be. In fact, it could be all of these factors, and more, contributing to your poor performance. But if we switched the exercise around so that you are now experiencing wild success, how quickly would you lock into one or two factors to define your high performance?

No matter how you slice it, chances are you won't be able to pinpoint the one thing that makes you successful. In other words, there are no "silver bullets" for success. No matter what your personality type is, or the knowledge and skill you posses, or any other factor you can come up with, one thing is for certain: You must continuously adapt to the world around you. Better yet, you must continuously learn if you want your success to be repeated.

CONSIDER THIS

Becoming successful today requires both knowing AND doing.

So how do you keep learning? To be more specific, how do you find time to learn about new products, stay on top of the competition, keep up with industry trends, update your customer relationship management [CRM] tool, maintain a constant flow of communication internally, show up to meetings on time, understand where each buyer is in the decision-making process, serve as the "face of the company," and keep up the momentum? From internally focused actions that require an immediate response to externally focused collaboration that must be strategically managed, how do you stay on top of it day after day? After all, it seems a little random and chaotic doesn't it?

Or to simplify the question, how do you manage the chaos of sales?

CHAOS—THE FINAL FRONTIER

That's right, we said it. Chaos—the final frontier. Sounds like science fiction, right? To be fair, there is a bit of science geek to it, but the bigger truth is if you are living in the reality of today's business, you are probably swimming in it. Chaos, that is.

If Daniel's story resonated with you at all, think about all the complexity you wrestle with in your business life (or Daniel does). Think about the complex set of influences found within the massive storm cloud that is called an economy. Identifying

BUILDING ON THE FOUNDATION

Chaos Theory

Chaos theory is a large part of this book, but don't let it scare you. Chaos theory doesn't mean that things are out of control. On the contrary, you'll find that chaos theory lets you harness the seemingly random activity around you.

According to the Merriam Webster dictionary, chaos theory is the study of the consequences of chaos and chaotic systems. In this book, we pull from chaos theory, organization behavior, management science, and an in-depth understanding of the sales profession to help you understand the consequences of chaos as you engage in a conversation with your customers.

One of the first scientists to comment on chaos was Henri Poincaré (1854–1912), a late-19th century French mathematician who extensively studied topology and dynamic systems. He explained, "It may happen that small differences in the initial conditions produce very great ones in the final phenomena. A small error in the former will produce an enormous error in the latter. Prediction becomes impossible." Unfortunately, the study of dynamic systems was largely ignored until long after Poincaré's death.

From where we sit, the science of chaos theory is now a required discipline for the study of the nature of professional selling.

Source: Encyclopedia of Business, 2nd ed.

those components and writing them down would yield a list that everyone is pretty familiar with:

- Globalization
- More cultural diversity in the buying and selling environment

- "Off-shoring" of jobs
- Challenges in corporate ethics and governance
- Rapidly evolving knowledge and information
- More use of technology and the Internet
- Multiple processes within the marketing, selling, and delivery functions
- Broader responsibilities across the organization when it comes to growing revenue
- Multiple organizational strategies leading to a need for fresh tactics

UNDERSTANDING THE CHAOS

Now, take it a step further. Look specifically at the world of selling. If you're a sales professional reading this book, you are living in a reality that is complex, confusing, and chaotic. Many of the tactics and strategies that have worked so well over the last few decades are no longer obtaining the results you need. But some salespeople are coping with the complexity around them—and winning.

So how do they do it? And how can we leverage their winning ways across the enterprise? Business leaders and executives regularly struggle to apply this understanding to more of the sales team. Sales VPs want to "replicate their best salespeople"—but can't. Technology vendors promise to help you sell more stuff—but don't. Consultants say that sales managers need to hire the right people—but there isn't a clear definition of what that means. Many of the approaches taken by executives, vendors, and suppliers just don't work in helping salespeople become more successful. Let's face it, if their approaches were working, there would be more ways for you to thrive in the sales profession, instead of getting burned out or tossed out of the profession.

UNDERSTANDING THE COMPLEXITY

BUILDING ON THE FOUNDATION

Complexity

There is an amazing amount of scientific evidence that proves every system has the potential to fall into chaos.

The primary frame for understanding complexity around us is dynamic systems theory, which is used to describe processes that constantly change over time (for example, the ups and downs of the stock market). When systems become dislodged from a stable state, they go through a period of oscillation, swinging back and forth between order and chaos. According to Margaret J. Wheatley (1994) in *Leadership and the New Science*, "Chaos is the final state in a system's movement away from order."

Sounds a lot like professional selling doesn't it?

Source: Encyclopedia of Business, 2nd ed.

How did the business world become so difficult to work in? It's the result of all of this increased complexity. Obviously, people are looking for ways to deal with complexity, but none of the methods, strategies, or tools we see so casually tossed about seem to actually help. Frankly, many of them just add to the complexity. The result? Instead of creating solutions, we hear a lot of really sophisticated, highly intellectual excuses. And you know what you can do with excuses in the business world, right?

As sales professionals ourselves, we grew tired of excuses and lame attempts by vendors, suppliers, and (dare we say it) even sales management to help us sell more. So we took matters into our own hands.

It began with the realization that complexity breeds chaos. And the greater the complexity, the greater the chaos. This set us on a whole new trajectory in our thinking about how we communicate with our buyers. You see, if you are able to understand the concept of chaos, you are then able to deal with the complexity around you so it doesn't have a big impact on your sales conversations. You have to be agile. You cannot deal with such massive waves of complexity with the Rules of Order. That would be like trying to organize the grains of sand on a beach. Have fun counting and stacking sand while the tide is rising. This is why all of those other so-called solutions are so ineffective. This is why many times salespeople have a hard time selling solutions. They presume the complexity goes away. Well, we have news for you. It will never go away. Welcome to the new reality.

We knew that if we could just erase everything that we pre-supposed about professional selling, if we could rethink everything that is involved in selling today and look through the lens of chaos, we could turn our understanding of the new reality into the ability to sell differently. And if we could sell differently, we could manage business differently. We could become agile—and turn our agility in the chaos to a distinct advantage. A very profitable advantage at that.

After literally years of research, trial, and error, we did it. We cracked the code. It started to become clearer when we identified three overwhelming forces of the new reality that most people have ignored. We then realized that if we could allow these forces to run their course in a way that embraced chaos, a new business philosophy emerged. The complexity stopped being so confusing and actually started making sense.

INTRODUCING THE THREE FORCES OF COMPLEXITY

Are you ready for the three forces? Well, strap yourself in and get ready for a bumpy ride, because the next few pages are going to upset someone somewhere—and that might even include you.

PAY ATTENTION

There are three overwhelming forces of the new selling reality. And most people have ignored them, or worse yet, not even noticed them.

Force 1: The Force of the Non-Linear

Number 1: The Force of the Non-Linear (decision making is not sequential). Or in slightly more inflammatory language, the sales funnel is dead—and it has been dead since 2004 when we first published an article in the *Washington Business Journal* on it. Oh, we can hear some of you now. That's heresy! That's foolish! Yeah...whatever. Before you start arguing with us, hear us out.

First, have you noticed how random your workday has become? How your customer makes decisions? The typical sales funnel is woefully inadequate at helping you keep up with the random nature of customer decision making. And if you think the sales funnel contains only one process that you are dealing with, you're forgetting about communication processes, marketing processes, planning processes, measurement processes, and delivery processes (to name a few). Are you willing to lump all these into one generic sales funnel or process? If you are, then you're at least five years behind the buyer who has a process for everything—from making a decision to identifying needs. Let's face it; anyone who is thriving in the sales profession today recognizes that decisions are no longer linear. Shoot, sometimes buyers don't even know why, what, or how they are supposed to be buying, but their job title has "purchasing" or "buyer" somewhere in the middle of it so, by golly, that's what they're going to do. They may bring you in just in time to negotiate your price in one instance, and then ask you to start all over and help them identify a need in the next. There is still a kind of decision-making process, but it just doesn't always follow a nice, neat straight line any more. And sales funnels are all about straight lines. Heck, they're even nicely packaged into a series of steps. How can a sales funnel accurately measure the rate of what goes in and what comes out the bottom when things enter halfway through the process? And what do you do with opportunities that actually grow after the initial point of purchase? And if you analyze what's being measured within the sales process (for example, number of calls, number of appointments, number of proposals) don't you think it seems a little one-sided for the sales team? More and more input is required from other parts of the organization to be successful in identifying and closing new business. For example, you might need input from the delivery team, solutions from the engineering team, pricing help from marketing, and data from a database in another country to even get a proposal out the door. It all requires alignment, and the sales funnel doesn't cut it anymore, especially when it comes to managing sales opportunities along the entire breadth of the customer's experience with your company (and we're not even talking about how the customer defines value yet!).

Speaking of opportunities, a sales funnel also does a pathetic job of identifying which opportunities are easy and which are hard. How many of you keep the really difficult prospects out of your funnel until you know they are going to be a guaranteed success? Or worse, you only go after the guaranteed successes to keep your closing rate high. We call it the China Syndrome.

A sales team for a large energy company in China was being evaluated for their closing rate. Guess what? They were closing almost 100 percent of their deals. And revenue was still below target. The Western expats in charge were confused. They pulled in some of their local talent and asked, "Why?" "The answer is simple," said the local managers. "Chinese culture puts a premium on managing reputation." The sales reps were not pursuing anyone who might actually say no because they didn't want to lose face. So how useful was the sales funnel in that scenario? Turn the mirror on yourself. How useful is your sales funnel in determining your success in the next business cycle?

CONSIDER THIS

How many sales funnels have you seen that have overly simplified the buyer decision-making process? Are you 100 percent reliant on the sales funnel? Really?

Still not convinced? Let us offer another bit of evidence. Have you ever heard of the 80/20 principle? The original concept was developed by Italian economist Vilfredo Pareto. But it wasn't until 1941 that Joseph M. Juran applied Pareto's idea to business.

Juran used Pareto's principle to identify that 80 percent of results came from 20 percent of the causes. We apply this to sales all the time. Eighty percent of your revenue typically comes from 20 percent of your customers (and sometimes even less). What happens when you put every possible opportunity into your sales funnel? You skew your data. Your sales funnel is full of noise. Chances are, if you are really honest, that 80 percent of what is in your sales funnel is just noise. It's not going to replace that big customer your company just lost. As a single account, they were worth 15 percent of your business locally. And some of you reading this are already freaking out about how you are going to make bonus next quarter without them.

BUILDING ON THE FOUNDATION

Joseph M. Juran was a 20th century management guru who launched the "managing for quality" revolution in manufacturing and whose work in Tokyo helped turn the label "Made in Japan" from a joke into a symbol of quality.

In 1937, he coined the Pareto Principle, also known as the 80/20 rule, which states that 80 percent of effects come from 20 percent of causes. As a theory it achieved a sort of universality that could be applied to almost anything, from 20 percent of customers buying 80 percent of products, to 80 percent of production errors being made by 20 percent of workers, etc.

According to the Juran Institute, "Millions of managers continue to rely on [the rule] to help separate the 'vital few' from the 'useful many' in their activities."

Source: Los Angeles Times

Let us also add some longer-term thinking to this point. Your executive leadership, if they're good, has identified strategic customer segments that they want you to focus on. Frankly, if you get it right, landing some of those deals will set you up for some really good results that will last quite a while. But if they are harder to acquire, will you put them in your funnel? Not if it messes up your closing rate, you say. Because, for many of you, that would mess up your bonus or your performance rating. Or even more likely, your manager will harass you because the strategic opportunity you put into your funnel is not moving fast enough (whatever that means) and in some cases will even advise you to take them out of your funnel (it looks bad leaving them in). Consequently, your funnel continues to be full of useless noise, and your executive leadership complains that the sales force can't execute the strategy. Well, based on this scenario, executing the strategy is not what you are being paid to do.

Face it. The forces of the economy today are non-linear. We do not believe that salespeople should be forced to operate solely in a sequential sales-funnel-type manner. It's too narrow, too constricting, too myopic, and too one-sided. (We've seen many sales funnels that don't even reference the customer!) Instead, we believe that salespeople should have a non-sequential process that enables folks to apply their skills to everything from the simplest to the most complex (and most profitable) conversations.

As a result, the focus of this book is to clearly give you a new (and yes, even scientific) approach to selling, one that embraces the non-linear and makes it a competitive advantage. But if you still want to use a sales funnel, enjoy the insanity.

Force 2: The Force of Full Value

The second force is the Force of Full Value (that is, evolving buyer expectations). Here's a little secret. The concept of buying has changed. Call it the natural order of the universe, or simply call it the impact of the Internet, but the people who buy have figured out how to access your greatest secrets. They know your prices, your products, your services, your capabilities, and your competitors, often even better than you do. They can read your marketing data before they even contact you, self-diagnose their needs (even if they are wrong), and bring you into the discussion only when they want to negotiate the deal. All because of the Internet and social networks.

BUILDING ON THE FOUNDATION

A social network is a community of individuals (or organizations) connected by one or more types of relationship (family, common interests, commerce, friendship, knowledge, status). Social network analysis is focused on uncovering the patterning of people's interactions.

Salespeople used to be the guardians of product and industry knowledge. We used to schedule appointments to share information with potential and current customers so that we could use the conversation to create influence. But now we've put everything onto our websites and given people the information before they even request it. The result? While buyers appreciate the open access and marketing can show some activity, the influence of the sales professional has shrunk, and in some cases disappeared. With the ability (and in some cases the all-out push) to order online, many buyers believe they don't have to interact with a salesperson at all, which only makes the efforts of a sales professional to get some face time seem unnecessary and perhaps even annoying.

CONSIDER THIS

Value isn't about your products and services. Today, value is about a business conversation that occurs at all levels of the organization so that you can drive the right outcomes for the customer—repeatedly.

At the same time, buyer expectations have evolved. Have you noticed how customers can complain about anything? Seriously, they can identify things that have absolutely nothing to do with the product or service you sold them, like complaints from other departments, invoice errors, and even their own poor business results (as if you were responsible for their business). And here you are, with voicemails and emails all saying the same thing. "Don't sell me anything else," they say. "Just protect the value of what you sold me already."

Did you catch that? "Protect the value"—not "sell me value," "promise me value," or "communicate the value." And by the way, your value is not what the Marketing group packaged up for your message either. In fact, they'll say, "That stuff is great on the website, and I read it earlier." So it's bigger than that. Much bigger than that.

Think of it this way. Professional selling should not be just the products and services you sell. We believe it should be able to help you keep up with what the buyer wants so that the experience of full value is not only achieved, but is repeated. What makes this so difficult is the way it must be achieved—through conversations between buyer and seller, with the full support of the selling organization. These conversations, conducted over time, create expectations that must be managed.

Oh, by the way, don't forget your job is to protect this definition of value, even if you're not quite sure what it is because the customer won't tell you.

And it's not just the conversations you'll have during the sales process. It's the conversations you'll have after the sale, which, by the way, is another reason why the sales funnel is dead—especially if yours ends with "deal closed." Today's buyer does not want you to disappear after he or she has bought something. Get this, buyers actually want you to stick around and deal with problems when they happen. Are they nuts? You don't do that. That's the job of Customer Service (or Accounting, the relationship manager, or Supply, or . . .). Well, get over it, because, as we warned you already, the ride is only going to get bumpier. Welcome to the new professional reality, where more and more sales professionals will find themselves covering the entire customer buying experience as part of an intensely complex buyer-seller relationship, all in the name of value. And, here's a little secret: We know several companies who have already aligned their sales force to this new reality. These companies now have one single point of contact for the entire customer experience because the customers demanded it. And yes, this single point of contact is the salesperson.

But we digress. . . .

Look at it this way. Randomly ask someone on your sales team whether she is spending enough quality time with customers. Ninety-nine times out of one hundred the answer will be "no." What's driving that result? Salespeople are having to manage the force of "full value." Well, come to find out managing the force of full value requires a lot of paperwork, documentation, tracking, internal meetings, project management, and general administrative "stuff" that never existed before. You need to rethink what it means to take care of your customers. Why? Because the definition of value, the "thing" that your customer has paid you for, has changed. In fact, the definition has actually grown. And all of this so-called extra stuff is now permanently part of your job. Bonus check not necessarily included.

Force 3: The Force of Community

Decision making is now a public event. It is no longer about the buyer and seller; it is about the buying community and the selling community as they intermingle to create connected agreement. Yes, it's true. The days of the "one decision-maker" are over—and they have been for a long time. Again, we have to give a nod to technology here and call it the buyer network. Buyer networks began when the Internet (and company intranet) became a part of everyday life and connected whole groups of people. These groups were able to be involved, positively and negatively, in the decision to buy. As a result, buyers have become extended networks. These networks can be simple or complex. Here's a real-life example:

A multi-national organization needed to make a buying decision on software. The staff of the corporate head office involved individuals from a combination of ten subsidiaries and wholly owned corporations as part of the buying network. There was no "one" decision-maker. In fact, each of the designees was appointed to a buying committee from the subsidiaries (forming a "sub-buying" network), while they still represented their own individual buying entity. The sales funnel was woefully inadequate to deal with the complexity of this type of deal (the sales funnel was stuck in "discover" phase for almost nine months!). Forecasting was a waste of time because the salesperson couldn't exactly determine when the deal was going to close. Managing the global buying network spanning four countries that was comprised of representatives from ten different buying networks was a full-time job. Compounding the issue was the multi-million-dollar size of the deal, multi-year agreements, and high expectations for quality, responsiveness, and ease of use.

CONSIDER THIS

You can't sell alone anymore. If you sell in a complex environment and believe the community isn't impacting your effectiveness as a seller, how often do you find yourself complaining about others getting in the way? Isn't it time to do something about that?

Pause. In the example above, think about what it took to close the sale. Obviously, we are talking both sides of the game here. Remember what we said in Force 2 about the sales professional being responsible for managing the force of full value? Well, we forgot to mention (actually we didn't, we were just setting you up for the sucker punch) that the responsibility goes two ways. For every vice president, engineer, accountant, purchasing agent, and maintenance technician on the buyer's side, there is a lawyer, sales director, inventory manager, marketing lead, and contract specialist on the seller's side. And everyone has a company-mandated job to do, even if it gets in the way of you trying to do your job in managing multiple buying networks across each customer experience.

Furthermore, each of these players constantly connect with their counterparts in other organizations. Make a mistake with one, and the offended party will electronically broadcast (or even Twitter) his displeasure throughout his network. Emails are sent as a formal record of your mistake so that, at the end of the day, if the deal goes south, someone can be blamed. And we're including folks on the same side in this behavior (anyone ever complain to your colleagues about the Legal team?).

To compound things, authority levels to make decisions are going higher and higher, often to folks who have nothing to do with generating revenue. In our buyer-network example above, staff at the corporate head office had to formalize and create the team. They had to set aside some corporate money and help coordinate quarterly meetings. And they had to poke, prod, and otherwise kick the subsidiaries to come up with most of the investment dollars. Just talking about the customer's perspective, this deal was spread across ten different organizations, with support money coming from headquarters. Who's "the buyer" now? And don't get us going on what it took internally to sell the deal.

As one experienced sales executive told us, "It's getting to the point where the average salesperson can't do his job any more without going to someone at the home office for final approval on the most basic of deals. And I always get nervous when Finance has the last say."

USING THESE FORCES TO OVERCOME COMPLEXITY

We believe that selling should not be focused on just the buyer-seller relationship. It should be enlarged to address the entire system that supports a series of sales conversations, while overcoming these three forces.

Perhaps the most frustrating part of this dynamic is that the salesperson is no longer in charge of the customer relationship, but the buyer is expecting him or her to be. Read that again. Salespeople are expected to represent the entire company from marketing to fulfillment and delivery, but they often don't have the power to do so. Still want to protect the full value that was sold? The silos in buying and selling communities make that all but impossible. Or, as we like to say, "Everything looks great on paper until people get involved."

How are you feeling right now? Did you know these things already, or did the moisture leave your mouth as you suddenly realized the cause of your pain? Honestly, if you have already identified any of these elements (the forces of the non-linear, full value, and community), good for you. But if you've never been able to put these dynamics into words . . . well, don't sweat it. We say that once you identify a problem it loses half of its strength. Feel better? Because the next question is the one that will hurt the most.

What are you going to do about it? Seriously, if the world of selling has changed, how are you going to change?

THREE CHOICES ALL SALESPEOPLE HAVE TO MAKE

The way we see it, you have three choices:

1. Work harder or
2. Work smarter using old tools or
3. Work smarter using a new perspective and new tools

Now, before you start answering the question, sit still for a moment while we calibrate a few things, especially the term "old." Waaaay back in the 20th century (chuckle if you want, but to today's generation, the 1980s and 1990s are just as irrelevant as the 1950s and 1960s), the theory was to play the numbers game in sales. You know. If you needed X result, just put in Y business leads and work the system based on the percentages of past success. In other words, work harder. And by the way, if you can't do it, we'll fire you and hire someone who can. Enter Alec Baldwin, stage right (anybody want a set of steak knives?).

Working harder and getting the same results you always have (which, for most of you, is "flat to declining") is the axiomatic definition of insanity. And you can try to work smarter, but if you are using the same old tools (even the sparkly technological ones), today's reality quickly transforms your smart work into old-fashioned hard work. It's like trying to chop wood with a dull axe blade. Not fun, and you are working even harder, only to obtain limited results.

> ## PAY ATTENTION
>
> You have three choices:
>
> 1. Work harder or
> 2. Work smarter using old tools or
> 3. Work smarter using a new perspective and new tools

THE DEMOGRAPHIC SHIFT IN SALES

In a way, they were right. Baby Boomers dominated the workplace. Their sheer numbers meant two things: First, there were hundreds of opportunities out there, because few people had actually connected with their market the way they could. There simply wasn't enough time in the day to do it all.

Second, replacing poor performers was easy. The "numbers game" also applied to workforce planning. Boomers were so plentiful that finding someone who was both good at what he did and dissatisfied with his current job wasn't too hard. People were always looking for greener grass (even if it was shiny and plastic).

Then a couple of things changed (well, actually a lot of things, but for the sake of getting to the point, let's focus on two). First, the creation of the Internet and its associated technology boom suddenly transformed access to the market exponentially. Seemingly overnight, people were mass emailing, multi-tasking, and BlackBerry-ing their workday into overdrive. The market matured just as fast, and brand new markets emerged explosively (especially Brazil, Russia, India, and China). We finally created a twenty-four-hour workday, seven days a week.

Second, Boomers grew older. They started filling out senior leadership roles and (worse) retiring. The next generation, Gen X, didn't have the numbers to support a strategy of "make it or you're fired." There just wasn't enough talent to go around, and the talent that was going around was far more cautious about shiny, artificial grass. Gen X'ers were not about to put everything into a workplace that sacrificed their private lives.

So Generation X started working smarter. They started focusing their activities in the market by blending communication technology with their work. They segmented the market into micro-segments, targeting where growth was easier and, if necessary, taking the business global through technology. Needed to talk with India, London, and San Francisco at the same time? No problem. Wanted to work from home, eliminating the wasted time of driving to and from work and to and from customers? Talk to IT. Want to interrupt someone who is in an important meeting? Just text the person (because you know she can't resist the urge to glance down at a vibrating phone).

Meanwhile, the Boomers (who were still running the show) quickly adopted the ideas and enlarged them to include cost-management plans to go with their revenue-generation plans (off-shoring, anyone?). The result? Both buyer and seller quickly made the operations side of the ball leaner than TQM in the 1980s, thus increasing demands on the sellers to be even more efficient for even less cost.

CONSIDER THIS

Of all the sales books you have read lately, which have really explained the complexities of selling? Are you still using 1980s or 1990s thinking in an attempt to solve New Millennium challenges? While the selling world is becoming more and more complex, many sales books are written to be overly simplistic and motivational.

And what is happening now? Boomers and Gen X are still running around, with Millennials joining the party in massive waves. The value of technology has become almost a burden. You no longer have the traditional refuge of being out of the office (you turned your home into the office, remember?), while the personal lives of the Millennials seems to be creeping into the workplace through, you guessed it, technology. And the so-called emerging markets are pretty darn sophisticated, while the "old" markets are even more chaotic than they were just a few years ago.

That leaves us with the choice to work smarter using a new perspective and new tools. Seriously, new means new. We are not talking about managing sales funnels. We are not talking about how to sell products, services, or solutions. And we are not even talking about sales as a function. We are talking about things that are bigger, more complex, and require a completely different way of looking at your business. We are talking about taking the forces of the non-linear, full value, and community and letting them carry you away. Are you ready for that?

If you just answered yes, then we cordially invite you join us in the chaos — Sales Chaos, that is.

Making It Stick

Diagnostic Tool: Evaluating the Forces You Encounter

This diagnostic is designed to help you analyze the three key forces found in this chapter against one of your key clients or customers. Let's see whether the forces are at play.

Simply answer "yes" or "no" to each of the following questions. To begin, make sure you pick one of your most important customers. By answering each question honestly, you will begin to understand the impact of the complexity around you.

Customer/Company Name: _____

Deal/Opportunity: _____

Evaluating the Impact of Force 1 – Non-Linear

1. Do you constantly have to adjust your approach to this customer based on external market forces and trends? _____

2. Is it common for you to adjust your schedule for this customer? _____

3. Does your sales funnel contain non-critical noise about this customer? _____

4. Do you believe your forecast for this customer has serious gaps in accuracy or information? _____

5. Does your sales process overly simplify how this customer actually makes buying decisions? _____

Evaluating the Impact of Force 2 – Full Value

1. Does your customer appreciate your involvement before and after the sale? _____

2. Is your customer's definition of value different from what you (and/or your company) define as a unique selling proposition? _____

3. Do you have to customize messages and actions often in order to position your value for this customer? _____

4. Does your customer complain about things that are outside of features and functions? _____

5. Does the number of administrative and "non-selling" activities impact the amount of quality time with this customer? _____

Evaluating the Impact of Force 3 – Community

1. Do you often find that more than one or two people are involved in the purchase decision and can say "no" (including those internal to your own organization)? _____

2. Do you find that you need to bring other people into the discussion in order to solve issues, problems, and concerns for this customer? _____

3. Do you often rely on others to facilitate an introduction in order to move the sale forward or acquire key information for this customer? _____

4. Do you believe you are well supported by your organization at the point of sale and beyond? _____

5. Do you wish you had more information flow internally to support your efforts with this customer? _____

Fundamentals of Sales Chaos: Butterflies

"What if the flap of butterfly's wings in Brazil set off a tornado in Texas?"

Edward Lorenz

INTRODUCTION

Jennifer was a successful salesperson by any standard. With ten years of industry experience under her belt, she had just walked into a multi-million-dollar customer portfolio with forty-five named accounts; only three of them were strategic. After two weeks, she had uncovered multiple customer issues, ranging from messed up invoices to implementations that were 120 days late. On top of that, Jennifer had identified that within thirty days she was going to lose several contracts that were up for renewal. Because she was just starting the new job, she shared the information with her boss. His response was, "Wow. It looks you like you have your work cut out for you; better get busy." When she responded that she might need some internal help, he told her, "Focus on what you can control. By focusing on what you can control, you will soon realize what you can and cannot do. You cannot fix the back office issues. You aren't responsible for the implementations. Find new prospects to fill in the revenue gap and you'll be fine."

What?!

Ok, so let's make sure we understand. The manager's answer to Jennifer's dilemma was to overcome chaos by narrowing her vision. Or, worse yet, survive chaos by ignoring it. Unfortunately, we have seen this type of response many times before. We're willing to bet you have too. Complexity isn't new. But the level of complexity that salespeople deal with today is much greater than it was five, ten, or twenty years ago. In Chapter 1, we talked about what complexity looks like. While many would argue that an individual's ability to handle the complexity around him can only be built over time, we don't necessarily agree. We think that the ability to manage the complexity can be learned much more quickly, if you understand how the complexity works.

CONSIDER THIS

You have to know and understand your role in handling the complexity. While many may choose to ignore their roles, ask yourself, and ask your customer, what role you should have in helping to navigate the complexity.

THE IMPACT OF COMPLEXITY

Because of the complexity of the business world, professional selling has evolved into a system. There are many people involved, and with that system, there are multiple factors at work. These factors are interconnected, and even adaptive. This means that you can push on one small of piece of the system and something that is seemingly unrelated will eventually react somewhere else. Every time. For example, reorganize the sales force, and the technology that supports it may become obsolete. Change a process, and the relationships that matter most may unintentionally become strained—or even healthier. It all depends on the change.

Unfortunately, we have seen many salespeople attempt to overcome the complexity of the system by trying to remove it. Or worse, ignore it. This approach creates even more challenges than you started out with, and we don't recommend doing that at all. On the other hand, people try to overcome the complexity by adding to it, as if that will magically make the system run more smoothly. Folks, more activity and more motivation aren't going to handle the complexity. Nether are more proposals or new technology, especially if they rely on linear thinking. The system won't allow it.

BUILDING ON THE FOUNDATION

Complex System

You've probably heard the phrase, "The whole is greater than the sum of the parts." Complex systems deal with the interconnected parts that, when taken together, become something different. Professional selling fits this definition, in that marketing, selling, and product groups can be managed separately, but together, they can generate revenue. The key is to treat them in totality as a system and not as separate parts.

So we have now backed you into a corner. You must now make one of two choices. Your first choice will be to run as fast as you can away from this reality that we are describing and deny what is going on around you. Instead of looking at what lies in the future, you can stubbornly cling to what you know from the past. The consequence of this choice is that you stay in the corner. Forever.

The second choice is to recognize the force of the non-linear in your system. In fact, we say that you should embrace this force of chaos. Become a student of the non-linear and use it to understand how your system works. The consequence of this choice is that you will transform the complexity that others struggle with into your own competitive advantage.

To us, the other choice makes the most sense. If you're going to jump into the ocean, you had better know how to swim, right? So you can imagine how sad it makes us when we watch salespeople all over the world who are swimming in an ocean of chaos, but who continue to convince themselves that they can make the ocean do what they want it to. We know it sounds crazy, but it's true. That's why we offered you a choice. If you choose to embrace the force of the non-linear, we'll save you literally years of wasted efforts and stress. We'll help you see the chaos as something that can be slowed and even harnessed. Your choice, your consequence.

PAY ATTENTION

The force of the non-linear will drive you to make one of two choices. One choice will be to run as fast as you can away from reality and deny what is going on around you. The other choice will be to embrace the world of Sales Chaos.

Are you ready to dig a little deeper?

THE NEED FOR THEORY

Please don't be like the sales manager in Jennifer's story. You just cannot look at the business world and put it into neat little boxes anymore. Get over it and change your mindset.

At the same time, we've all experienced the fresh-from-university new hire (or worse, the fresh-from-university consultant) who intellectually describes how we are "doing it all wrong" and how we need to apply Theory X and Model Y to put our business in those neat little boxes that make perfect sense while sitting under the gleaming lights of the executive office. That's about when we shove him into a car, take him to see a real customer, and leave him stranded to hack it out with a buyer who eats fresh-from-university kids for lunch. If we're nice, we come back later and pick up the pieces.

The "real world"—as seasoned businesspeople so delicately refer to it—doesn't fit into a PowerPoint deck and is far more brutal than theories and models. We completely agree—to a point. You can go ahead and chuck out all of the theories and models that try to put the real world into little boxes. But a word of caution: Don't ignore the theories and models that help you see patterns in the chaos. Lenses, models, and theories that help you sort through complex situations, manage relationships, and keep up with evolving market conditions are absolutely necessary in the business world. You'd be foolish to think that selling isn't complex enough to actually need some of that stuff (if only to keep your sanity).

So where were we? Ah, yes, going a little deeper.

PAY ATTENTION

Don't ignore theories and models that help you see patterns in the chaos.

CHAOS THEORY–SENSITIVITY TO INITIAL CONDITIONS

It's time to introduce you to the actual science behind chaos theory. We know. We're starting to sound like science geeks again. But there is no other choice here. Chaos theory is driven by the force of the non-linear, and you have to grasp it if you are going to slow the chaos around you. Here's the good news. By your understanding chaos theory, the chaos around you will actually make sense. Chaos will become a beautiful thing. And you will wonder why you tried looking at the world of business through the lens of order in the first place.

Let's start with some background. Chaos theory started in the late 1800s. Mathematicians knew that linear systems could not accurately describe things that relied on non-linear dynamics. In other words, they knew the universe didn't always move in straight lines.

BUILDING ON THE FOUNDATION

BUILDING ON THE FOUNDATION

Dr. Edward Lorenz

Edward Lorenz was a mathematician and meteorologist at the Massachusetts Institute of Technology who loved to study weather. With the advent of computers, Lorenz saw the chance to combine mathematics and meteorology. He worked to build a mathematical model of the weather and built a mathematical model to determine whether a computer could predict long-term weather patterns using his calculations. He ran one weather model simulation on his machine. He then wanted to extend the forecast, so he added a second simulation with the same parameters and conditions of the first. The predicted weather pattern should have seamlessly flowed into the second simulation.

Instead, the trajectories quickly diverged.

The problem: a rounded decimal number. Dr. Lorenz realized that the computer stored numbers to an accuracy of six decimal places but, to save space, printed out results shortened to three decimal places. So, for example, 0.310625 became 0.311. For the second simulation, he had used the shortened figure.

Even this minute discrepancy drastically altered the forecast.

Tiny changes, in effect, could have catastrophic, and often unpredictable, consequences. And they made perfect predictions of weather, even through the emerging power of computers, impossible. Exact measurements of all the conditions could be upset by one small event, such as the flap of a gossamer wing.

The development of this theory changed not only how scientists viewed the prediction of weather, but also had applications in such sciences as fluid dynamics

Source: The Boston Globe, 2009

Enter Dr. Edward Lorenz, meteorologist. It was 1961, and Ed was running some numbers through a computer to study weather prediction, a classic example of a non-linear dynamic. He decided to take a shortcut and entered the decimal .506 instead of the full .506127 in the middle of the sequence to save some time. The result? A completely different weather scenario. Ed was onto something huge, and it took a computer to show how much assumption was really going on.

You see, the tiniest of variance, introduced into any non-linear process, can create massive changes down the road. Which is why the weather should only forecast a week out—at the most. Any longer, and the data is so vulnerable to change that it is virtually worthless. Anyone who has ever tried to plan a big golfing event knows exactly how true that can be.

CONSIDER THIS

Have you ever noticed how everything looks great on paper, until people get involved? Many times, the activities we accomplish yield a completely different outcome than we were expecting. In selling, is there really a way to say that D follows C, and C follows B with certainty? The goal is to identify the forces at play so you can plan accordingly. That's where chaos theory comes in.

Look at it another way. It's a perfectly normal thing to assume that, on an average day, every airplane that takes off will start at point "A" and go to point "B" as planned. But how much can go wrong if you change any one of the variables by just the tiniest of fractions (such as arrival time, weather conditions, air traffic congestion, or that person in aisle 12 who keeps trying to shove his luggage into a space that won't hold any more even as the scheduled departure time ticks into the past)? Somewhere, somehow, a certain percentage of the day's travel will be screwed up. In fact, each slight variance can create ripple effects further down the line. Hopefully, somewhere along the line someone identifies the variability and copes with it. But what happens when (a) variability isn't recognized or (b) variability isn't handled in a proactive way? In short, bad things can happen, and sometimes people get hurt, even when none of it was intentional. This is what we mean when we say that non-linear forces and dynamics are constantly at work.

THE BUTTERFLY EFFECT

This is what Ed had discovered. It's a concept that is now called the Butterfly Effect, and it plays a major part in Sales Chaos Theory. The concept is easy to understand, and it's usually asked in the form of a question. If a butterfly flaps its wings in Brazil and introduces a minor fluctuation in the non-linear weather pattern, will the action of its wings set off a tornado in Texas? While this might sound like scientific silly talk, it's an important consideration to bring into the business world. In this case, we are not talking about minor fluctuations in temperature or wind patterns. We're talking about the reactions of human beings to the world around them.

BUILDING ON THE FOUNDATION

The butterfly effect explains a foundational premise of chaos theory. The butterfly effect explains that a chaotic system is very sensitive to initial conditions. The phrase was coined by Edward Lorenz in a talk he gave at the 139th meeting of the American Association for the Advancement of Science in 1972, titled "Does the flap of a butterfly's wings in Brazil set off a tornado in Texas?"

Source: J. Gleick. *CHAOS: Making a New Science.* New York: Penguin Books, 1987.

We'll spare you any of the scientific justification and analysis of the "butterfly effect," but here's the big takeaway. The butterfly effect has more to do with sensitivity to initial conditions than with fixing ramifications. In other words, minor fluctuations in early stages create major disruptions later on. *If you can watch for these fluctuations as they occur, you can proactively avoid creating major disruptions.*

Which reminds us of a sales scenario we call the "Australia deal."

In Australia, a highly competitive and hard-working salesperson was trying to close a deal with a big mining outfit somewhere in the Outback.

Pause. How many non-linear dynamics do you see in this sentence? There are at least eight. Check it out:

1. *Australia.* Culture, economy, and politics are just a few of the things that create market influences that drive salespeople crazy. An Aussie will understand some of these subconsciously, but what do you want to bet that this bloke wasn't a student of the market?

2. *Highly competitive.* Yeah, that's right, Sherlock, our player hated to lose and would "sometimes" skip doing his homework on the details to get a victory.

3. *Hard-working.* Frankly, most people love this variable with the exception of the times that the hard-worker has been burning the candle at both ends. It creates risk, the kind that most companies hate and don't want to take responsibility for, especially if they are the ones creating an environment of overwork. See any non-linear behavior in that environment?

4. *Salesperson.* Admit it. Salespeople are different. The purpose of this relationship was generating revenue. Here's a question for you. How do you think salespeople are treated differently than, say, technical engineers when they show up at a customer's location? The customer introduces non-linear behavior as well.

5. *Close a deal.* It could have been to end the quarter or end the year. Regardless, the player in this story was adding to the chaos created by his highly competitive personality with short-term thinking.

6. *Big*. This one is easy. Big companies usually mean complex and often confusing decision making. Our customers deal with the same garbage that we do.

7. *Mining*. Think "technical requirements galore." And add some ego to it, because miners have egos (in case you've never met one before).

8. *Outback*. Here come the logistical nightmares. Imagine mile after mile (or kilometer after kilometer) of nothing. Just dirt, grass, and millions of little termite mounds. Transporting supplies safely, accurately, and on time in this environment is the very definition of non-linear dynamics. Plus, the salesperson only came out this far into the middle of nowhere to close the deal, remember?

Ok, back to the story. Our salesperson happily closes the deal, with two slight twists. Instead of shipping the typical packaging of mining supplies on the typical delivery schedule, the mining company asks for two small things. They ask for slightly customized packaging delivered on a different day. "No problem," said the salesperson. The math in his head said the deal was worth $50K a year (and a sweet piece of business). The changes were so minor that he figured the costs would be minimal. But he was too busy cashing his commission check in his head instead of thinking about the butterflies he had just introduced. And here they all come—masses and masses of them. By the time these two "minor" changes were put into action (packaging and delivery), the supplier lost $150,000 every year of the deal to collect the annual $50,000 that the salesperson "won." And the worst part of it? The salesperson was paid for closing the deal as part of his compensation.

THE BUTTERFLY EFFECT–SALES VERSION

So the butterfly exists in professional selling today. We've seen it sneak up on salespeople many times. We've also seen it leveraged by great salespeople who always end up staying in front of trends. Have you ever dealt with your own butterfly effect? Yeah, you're probably trying to digest one right now. The butterfly effect is constantly at work in the world of professional selling. But not all butterflies are dangerous.

CONSIDER THIS

The butterfly effect can be a positive force with many of your clients. Working diligently, you can begin aligning people and processes to achieve alignment to your strategy. Just remember: This may require patience and understanding that don't necessarily fit into your company's quarterly focus. Understanding this will help you balance the short-term and long-term alignment you need. Introduce new butterflies now, and catch them later.

Here is a list of the four most common places you will find butterflies:

- *People:* Shift the decision-makers around, introduce a new competitor, or reorganize the purchasing department—all of these people-related examples show fluctuations that can create major disruptions later. And butterflies can be found on your own team as well.

- *Time:* Move the deadline forward, push a critical meeting back, or even get hit by the normal calendar of business (summer vacations anyone?), and the time-related butterflies will pop out of the woodwork.

- *Energy:* Apprehension toward a new product or process, fatigue from a extended period of hard work, or even an old-fashioned sense of dissatisfaction are all examples of energy in the world of selling. Leave any one of those energies alone and it could transform into a butterfly overnight.

- *Resources:* Generally speaking, we are talking about equipment, location, and money. A minor fluctuation with any one of these and the ripples that follow could derail an entire negotiation or the implementation of an agreement.

An easy way to remember this list is the acronym PTER: People, Time, Emotions, and Resources. We have given you some simple examples, but feel free to add your own. The key is to remember that you can proactively look at any sales situation and run through this acronym to see whether any butterflies are potentially gathering. You can also look at a gathering tornado and deconstruct how it started developing with the same PTER factors. If you can see the butterflies, you can determine which ones need your influence to keep the tornado from becoming a reality. If the butterflies cannot be influenced, at least make a plan to avoid getting hurt by the tornado that they are creating. Make sense? We hope so.

BUTTERFLIES ARE EVERYWHERE

It is essential to grasp what the butterfly effect teaches us. In today's business reality you must remember the butterflies. They are always appearing where you least expected them, and you must identify them when they do. But you cannot control them. Control is a myth. Seriously, it's a myth. You can't *control* the market, the weather, your customers, your co-workers, etc. All you can do is *influence*. Therefore, you must choose where you want to put your influence: on the butterflies or on the tornadoes.

PAY ATTENTION

You must choose where you want to put your influence: on the butterflies or on the tornadoes.

Too often, we see sales professionals completely flip out because they are trying to rope a tornado. If that's you, stop doing it. It's a freakin' tornado! Tie things down, get some cover, and clean up the mess afterward. You are too late anyway. Quit trying to blame other people or other departments. What you should have done was look for the butterflies and accounted for them before things got out of hand. Sadly, too many salespeople tell us that they were simply too busy to look for butterflies, and besides, they were "just" butterflies. Again, if you like this kind of insanity, put the book down. Clearly, we are not the kind of help you need.

For the rest of you, make sure that you grasp the butterfly effect completely. You only have a limited amount of influence. How and when you choose to use it is perhaps one of your greatest choices during the working day (and we'll argue that it works just as well at home).

MIRROR MOMENT

Where is your time going? Are you proactively working with butterflies or are you reactively chasing tornadoes?

Remember, the non-linear abounds. Everything looks great on paper until people are involved. If you try to look at your business with a linear mindset, you are going to miss a lot of butterflies and waste a lot of time.

'Nuff said.

Making It Stick

This tool will help you identify the butterflies you may be consistently finding (or ignoring). The list below will help you start.

Remember, a tornado is any major disruption to your customer relationship. Think of a customer or account where you may be experiencing a tornado now (or in the past). Determine which of the following butterflies contributed to your tornado:

People

Time

Energy

Resources

Step 1: Which of these can I influence? (*Note:* if you cannot influence anything, let the tornado pass.)

Step 2: Of the butterflies I can influence, how should I minimize their negative impact?

Step 3: Given the butterflies I have identified, which new butterflies (people, time, energy, resources) should I now introduce in order to keep the tornado from forming again?

Fundamentals of Sales Chaos: Anchor Points

"You can't always control the wind, but you can control your sails."

Tony Robbins

INTRODUCTION

Have you ever been in a storm? Hold your horses, champion, we're not talking about some business analogy (yet). We mean a real, hold your seat, clench your teeth, and pray like crazy storm – on open water? You know, where the boat jerks upward, starts to roll, then slams back down onto the water so hard that your bones hurt.

Being in a storm like this is scary as heck, and the first thing you look for is how far away from land you are. Sometimes, you cannot get back to your home port, so you search for a small bay or inlet where you can at least get away from the worst of the waves and the wind and drop an anchor. If you know your stuff, you drop another anchor off the other end of the boat so that your boat doesn't spin around just one point. In the best-case scenario, your boat can drop four anchors (two off the bow and two off the stern).

There's a lot to the science of anchoring beyond just finding a place to chuck a large weight with a rope over the side of the boat. You have to have a good anchor, it needs to be solid, and your anchor has to be the right type for the conditions of the seabed. You also have to pick a location where you can stay in one spot without bumping into anything. That means you have to stay away from obstacles you can see on top of the water, as well as obstacles you cannot see under the water. You also should anchor in a location that isn't inside any major shipping lanes. (*Note:* Large vessels take a long time to stop and turn!) And you have to have the right length of rope and chain between the anchor point and your boat. Despite all of this, the most important aspect of anchoring, and the reason why there are so many necessary requirements, is to make sure your anchors are securely connected to the seabed. That's why folks drop more than two anchors in case one pulls loose or the boat is dragged due to the fierce weather conditions.

Storms are a perfect example of chaos theory in action. Elements of the storm, such as wind, water, and temperature, all make reacting to conditions extremely difficult. Small changes in either can create major challenges for you. And every little mistake in coping with the environment around you can create major disruptions that you may have to deal with later.

THE POWER OF NON-LINEAR FORCES

By now you recognize that the power of non-linear forces is beyond any one person's control. You can't control the uncontrollable, especially during the series of sales conversations. But there is hope. Even in such random conditions as tides, weather patterns, other vessels, etc., there are common points of order and information. For example, while the sea is raging, the seabed is secure. As long as you attempt to anchor in a place that is shallow enough, your anchor will reach the bottom and be secure. This type of thinking can really help your sales conversations stay anchored to the buyer's definition of value. Once you can find and secure the anchor points, you can begin to understand (and even harness) the chaos around you.

FINDING THE PATTERNS

To go a step further, chaos theory actually defines this principle. The technical term is "pattern density." Think of it as chaotic motion swirling around common points. It's what keeps the chaos from spinning out of control and becoming completely random without any rhyme, reason, or repetition. You see, chaos will eventually provide you anchor points you can use before, during, and after your sales conversations—and it will only let you drift so far. In other words, the chaos will always return to those pockets of density to create patterns that actually mean something. In fact, the more you know about chaos, the more patterns you will begin to see. In our example of the storm, if you could go above the boat and look at the waves, you would see a pattern in how the waves were moving. You would see the same thing in the air above the storm. Have you ever stared out the window when flying above the clouds? If you look closely, you will find a pattern in the clouds.

BUILDING ON THE FOUNDATION

Pattern Density

Pattern density is formed when patterns are created. These patterns are created by chaotic motion swirling around common points. Pattern density is what keeps the chaos from spinning out of control and becoming completely random without any rhyme, reason, or repetition.

INTRODUCTION TO THE ANCHOR POINTS

If you examine what it takes to succeed in professional selling today, you can find patterns around four common areas. Think of them as the anchor points required to sell in chaos. If you are caught in a chaotic storm of buying and selling organizational (or individual) disruption, these anchor points will always provide you a pattern to come back to. And with that pattern firmly understood, you can have the kind of security you and your organization need to survive the storm. But wait a second. Survive is the wrong word. We mean *thrive*, as in "kicking your competition's backside and actually enjoying the storm" thriving.

Picture this. Bob was the newly appointed VP of sales in a mid-sized technology company. At this point, he'd been in the industry for fifteen years. The company was struggling to acquire new customers, and existing customers were leaving at an alarming rate. Bob's goal was to turn the revenue acquisition efforts around and help the organization survive in a tough economy (sound familiar?). Bob had no real understanding of Sales Chaos, but he was living it every day. He'd seen other companies face the same dilemma, but now he was in charge. Within the first few days of taking the job, it quickly became apparent that he had some major obstacles to work with.

The company had gone through the rare instance of splitting and rejoining years later. The result was a fragmented sales culture built on differing processes, priorities, and attitudes. The data management system was strained by, how shall we say, inconsistent usage (which only screwed forecasting up on a monthly basis). The marketing strategy was less than ideal, with the all-too-common approach of design—launch—aim (with no follow-up). Highly compensated salespeople were essentially glorified account maintenance reps, and Bob's competition was quickly catching up to his company's once industry-leading technology.

To make matters worse, some folks in human resources were spending precious resources on external consultants who were hired to provide sales training, even though the problems in the sales organization had little to do with what his people were supposed to know.

Bob had enough experience to know that he needed to look at the whole sales system, and he was actually poised to start embracing the chaos. He didn't have a solid understanding of systems, chaos theory, or complexity theory, but he knew that the problems he faced required him to approach the whole thing at one time. Unfortunately, an end-of-year adjustment to his sales projections drastically cut whatever chance he had to think strategically and holistically. He suddenly began reacting to the chaos around him by approaching each dilemma individually. He still had hope that his plan would succeed, but a month later, his sales numbers simply collapsed. Bob stopped looking for patterns in the chaos and gave up. Instead of continuing to wrestle with the unknown in order to identify a new way to manage his business, he gave in and went back to the old tools that he was familiar with, pushing the familiar levers of "work harder" and "motivate more." Without even realizing it, he was dooming the turnaround he was desperate to achieve. Multiple restructures, layoffs, and motivational speeches later, people were wondering whether they had hired the right guy.

You see, on one hand, all of this was completely Bob's fault. And on the other hand, it wasn't really his fault at all. You see, Bob felt that he couldn't do everything by himself and that he needed his entire sales organization to be responsive, proactive, and competitive. He wanted his whole team to be agile. But realistically speaking, the only way to ensure that type of action and adaptation was to take the time to identify patterns. And to do that, he needed to make sure his anchor points were secure (we know, we know, being agile by being anchored sounds contradictory–but keep reading). In the midst of a chaotic and seemingly random storm, he had to anchor the sales organization down so that it was stable enough to respond to his leadership. And, as captain of the ship, he completely ignored this responsibility.

Could you have done better? Would you know how to find the anchor points? Did you see them in the story you just read? Here are the anchor points we see:

- Sales fundamentals
- Sales processes
- Sales relationships
- Sales technology

The Impact of Anchor Points

Pause. Don't go lightly through this section. In fact, when one of us (Brian) first discovered that he had these anchor points to leverage, he was able to transform himself from first-time, newbie sales rep into nationally ranked, top-performing sales professional within three years. The other one of us (Tim) has consistently used them to stabilize and accelerate the transformation of sales organizations all over the world. They are not just generic talking points. Whether you are a player in a greater organization or the leader of the organization, these anchor points are the absolutely most essential ingredients to help you and your sales team members have great conversations with customers. If you can actually do more than talk about these four anchor points, you will turn chaos into an advantage and agility into something tangible.

All right, let's get back to defining the anchor points. Just for kicks, we'll use Brian's story as the backdrop.

PAY ATTENTION

If you can actually do more than talk about the four anchor points, you will turn chaos into an advantage and agility into something tangible. The four anchor points are (1) fundamentals, (2) processes, (3) relationships, and (4) technology.

Anchor Point 1: Sales Fundamentals

Let's begin the discussion with sales fundamentals: *what you're doing.* Brian spent a great deal of time defining his personal selling approach and the essential elements required for successful selling. He interviewed some of the high performers in the organization he worked for. He worked hard at finding out what his buyers wanted. But to be most effective, he had to separate the many aspects of his job so he could focus on driving the transaction itself—or else the sale wouldn't happen.

In fact, when he used the transaction as a filtering lens, he was quickly able to see the seabed beneath the raging storm. He could see what was vital to his success, and what was not. By freezing the transaction in specific moments in time, Brian was able to see all of the variables at work in that frozen moment. The most important element Brian saw was the customer's problem as it related to his or her buying process. The transaction wouldn't happen if the buyer didn't have a problem to solve—right? With that transaction (and that customer problem as the design point), he would then research the science necessary to influence as many of those variables as possible.

> ## CONSIDER THIS
>
> Using the customer as the design point means under-standing the one-to-one dialogue that needs to occur at the point of sale. It also means working backward all the way to the initial need as defined by the buyer. It is within this initial need that the definition of value is created.

Brian was able to determine what happened during the overall sale, why it happened, and how to avoid any missteps in the future. More importantly, he could gauge how well he was doing. Ultimately, it led to a realization that he had to develop some underlying skills that had nothing to do with the transaction process itself, yet they had everything to do with how the customer solves his or her problem and defines value. But we're getting ahead of ourselves—that'll come in a later chapter.

Anchor Point 2: Sales Processes

Brian also discovered something else on the seabed: *how to do it.* To accomplish this, he worked hard on fully understanding what occurred between buyer and seller during the series of conversations that took place. As a result, he was able to more clearly identify customer problems, find new problems that he (and his customers) never knew existed, and therefore complete more transactions. Between the loads of books and articles he read and the everyday experiences he was constantly pulled into, he found that a series of repeatable steps consistently culminated in a transaction. The kicker? These steps weren't "sale steps"; they were customer buying process steps. Or better yet, they were problem-solving steps. If he was lucky, these conversations could be supported by a linear process, as he had expected and as he was trained (his company sales funnel had five steps). More often than not, the conversations he had with his customers looped around, overlapped, and jumped all over the place, especially when there was more than one decision-maker or influencer involved.

CONSIDER THIS

Think about how people make purchase decisions. Rarely does their buying process fit nice and neatly into the sales funnel. Their buying decision-making process can be sequential or, during the course of a conversation, the decision-maker can loop back on him- or herself. Sometimes the decision-maker will bring up other seemingly random points, or even add others to the process late in the game. Buyer decision making can be confusing. The key is to focus on the customer's problem and then understand how they make a purchase decision once they have decided to buy. To do that, you can leverage the anchor points to stay in front of the process.

Even so, Brian began to see the various process patterns as they developed and could make sure that the conversations added value for the customer. By analyzing how sales work was accomplished in relation to the buyers' processes, he was able to work better with others on the team (especially his sales manager), regardless of where they were in the broader sequence of the conversation, while handling his own workload more effectively. As products, solutions, and customer requirements continued to become more complicated, Brian's foundation of fundamental sales processes was in place to cope with the increasingly higher levels of complexity.

By the way, did you see that? We said sales processes (as in more than one). There are more processes to manage than people realize (we'll explain that later). Understandably, this may be a little confusing. In one breath, we're telling you that buyers are often thinking in ways that cannot be described with straight lines, but we're also explaining about generating consistency in your sales processes at the same time. Don't processes require linear thinking? This is a contradiction, isn't it?

It's important to remember that the buying and selling processes we're talking about are grounded to a transaction and, much more specifically, to the customer's problem, there are also multiple factors at work that can influence the successful outcome of any given sales meeting. All of these extra factors add to the chaos. And because no single process can take the full buyer experience into account, lumping everything into one process (like a sales funnel) can't help you. What can help you are the multiple processes that exist to harness the chaos at any given moment.

Think of the waves and clouds we described earlier. Each one may not be in perfect and symmetrical order, but the overall picture clearly shows multiple patterns repeating themselves. Processes fit inside the patterns to help you harness them, but you can never force a pattern to appear simply because you are following a process. There is too much complexity at work in the environment around you.

Anchor Point 3: Sales Relationships

With the *what* and *how* figured out, a third anchor point quickly became apparent: *who you are working with*. Brian became more focused on the various relationships he needed in order to define and deliver value to the customer. Brian was thrust from being focused on transactions to being focused on relationships, both externally and internally. That change had a dramatic effect on his role as a sales professional, transforming his approach from "make everyone like you" into strategically defining who would take his time, both clients and co-workers.

> ## CONSIDER THIS
>
> If you're a salesperson, you need to realize that a large portion of your sales job is now comprised of working internally to your organization. In order for your customers to derive the value they are expecting, you will have to work internally (more often than not).
>
> While a large portion of your time may be focused internally, just remember that the rest of your time should be focused on having valuable conversations with external clients.

As those strategic relationships were established, buyers expanded their discussions beyond limited issues and needs. They began looking to Brian for solutions to business problems, as opposed to purchasing products and services from him and then brushing him away to manage their own implementations. As a result, Brian began helping his buyers facilitate their own buying decisions. He became a stronger problem-solver while engaging multiple stakeholders so that they were not subject to the whims of every decision-maker. He could actually coordinate his relationships with other members of the sales team to determine how they were brought into the discussion. Instead of just bringing in more folks for his customers to like, he could use their input to guide the various steps of the decision-making experience for his most valuable and complex customer relationships.

Anchor Point 4: Sales Technology

Another anchor point in the seabed that Brian discovered was trickier to find. He could see it, but it would randomly disappear and come back again. At first he thought it was just technology, but that wasn't it. Sure, the anchor point was embedded in technology, but it was really about *how to manage information flow.*

It is commonly accepted that technology is supposed to help you speed up your reaction time to market trends, keep you abreast of important industry and customer news, and develop a more solid understanding of your buyers. But Brian quickly discovered that, although personal computers, handheld devices, and customer relationship management systems promised to help him stay on top of the chaos that swirled around him, the mere presence of technology, by itself, was just an empty shell. The real key to managing the entire buyer experience was what the technology brought him — information.

It is said that information leads to knowledge, knowledge leads to skill, and skill leads to expertise. Without information, there is no learning. So what did Brian learn about? He learned who was talking to his customers, what they were talking about, and what his customers were saying in return. This kind of information was the lifeblood of his business. For example, if customer service, field support, or marketing were going to connect with his most important clients, Brian had to create a way to track it. Enter technology.

CONSIDER THIS

The real key to managing the buyer experience is information. Information helps salespeople learn. And learning leads to agility.

Once Brian configured his use of technology around information flow, the anchor point stopped randomly disappearing. The "when" of selling went from being too late (or not at all) to just in time, and sometimes even early. In other words, technology helped Brian go from reactive to proactive because he could anchor into sales information. Information was now moving at the speed that the IT guys had originally promised.

USING ANCHOR POINTS TO SEE PATTERNS

Taken together, these anchor points provided enough stability for Brian to do his job and thrive in a chaotic and seemingly random business storm. And the great thing about it is that each of these anchor points has been used to help a multitude of folks to obtain the same positive results over and over again.

Here's the tricky part. If you want to do more than wildly float around these anchor points, if you want to transform stability into agility, you have to tie into the anchor points in the right order. As we said earlier, process still exists in the middle of the chaos, and if you don't follow this process, you will only make the chaos worse.

THE ORDER MATTERS: SECURING THE ANCHOR POINTS

In case you missed it, we have already given you the process. That's right, the order in which we described the four anchor points is the order in which they must be understood and secured. It all starts with the *fundamentals*, then the *processes*, followed by *relationships* and *technology*. Makes complete sense doesn't it? Then why the heck do so many well-intentioned people screw it up? (Get ready, because we are about to poke some people who make ridiculously high salaries.)

We've talked about the China syndrome and the butterfly effect. We'd now like to introduce you to the "Intelligence Trap." A wise man once said, "In business, you have intelligent people and smart people. I'll take smart over intelligent any day of the week." What he meant was that many people may have nice university degrees (and we're not mocking that—we're both grad school alumni ourselves) that are loaded with theory and packed with educated arguments. But they don't know the first thing about how a real business works, especially how to actually sell something. Instead, they over-think what it takes to be successful in the eyes of a customer. They are distracted by the overly complex and other noncontributing "essentials." Or worse, they think that their intelligence can overrule just about anything, even a chaos storm. They honestly believe that their intelligence will counteract market dynamics, human behavior, and even old-fashioned luck.

The biggest threat inside the intelligence trap is the kind of distorted mental loop that occurs to folks who are caught in it. It typically goes something like this:

> *"I am intelligent. I have succeeded in academic studies and have the degree(s) to show it. I have even succeeded in the workplace and have the job title to prove it. Because I am intelligent, I am able to understand and manage complex things. I should always be successful because, fundamentally, I am intelligent. If I am not being successful, it's not my fault. It must be the fault of the less-than-intelligent people I am forced to work with. I do not need to listen to their ideas or feedback. Rather, they need to work harder at implementing my plans because my plans are intelligent, because I created them, and I am intelligent."*

Ever see this kind of flawed logic in action? If you are in the sales profession, you've probably seen it far too often. Somehow, these intelligent people are the ones who are put in charge of keeping the ship from getting smashed in a chaotic storm. Do they even know that they have anchor points to rely on? The smart ones do.

Why, then, do major corporations drop a ton of money to implement customer relationship management (CRM) systems on a sales organization that has no standardized customer processes that actually work? Why does HR need to roll out competency frameworks when salespeople have to spend their own money to obtain the kind of training that they actually need to be successful? Why does the sales organization need to go through a workforce reduction when the survivors will inherit an organization that is still going to be ad hoc, confused, and plagued with limited information flow?

You cannot leverage the power of sales technology until you have your sales fundamentals, sales processes, and sales relationships on track. You can't even leverage the power of sales processes as an anchor point if you haven't already tied into sales fundamentals. What good are your processes if the fundamentals that they rely on are not in place? In other words, who cares if you can put data into a CRM system if you are not good at selling?

PAY ATTENTION

You cannot leverage the power of sales technology until you have your sales fundamentals, sales processes, and sales relationships on track. Each level builds upon the previous.

Spending your precious time and resources to tie into anchor points is only a smart decision when the other anchor points have been secured in the right order. Spending your precious time and resources to tie into anchor points simply because some executive decided that it was the part of this year's "to-do" list is a sure sign you are caught in the intelligence trap. It will only accelerate the chaos that currently exists and could literally be blocking your ability to find, and tie into, your anchor points. Considering today's economy, can you afford to sacrifice your potential revenue for busywork?

THE NON-LINEAR REALITY OF BUSINESS

Anything that is non-linear is chaotic, and our own research and experience tell us there are no linear sales organizations any more. Trust us when we tell you that we know that your selling organization is chaotic. Multiple reorganizations, new management teams, new products, and new compensation plans are the yearly norm. The non-linear and random business environment is not going away any time soon.

What can you do?

We'll argue that you can set yourself up to thrive in the chaos by starting with your fundamentals. Define what you are supposed to be doing and cover your basics. Then add some standardization to your processes. Identify how your customers actually need you to behave so that you can define what you should do. At this point, you should have enough consistency to take a hard look at your relationships, both internally and externally. Find out which relationships are most important and which are receiving too much attention. Get these relationships operating the way they need to. Cultivate these relationships based on priority, not noise. Once you have your relationships in a place that actually drives the best use of your time, accelerate your effectiveness with solid information flow using technology. Make information flow to and from the places that matter most—even if it includes bad news. You don't want surprises!

Making Agile Adjustments

We almost forgot. There's one more lesson we can take from Brian's story. Once Brian had secured his four anchor points, the randomness and complexity around him didn't go away. It actually got worse. What did Brian do? He had to make adjustments. He had to reset a couple of anchors to make sure that he was responding to the chaos and maintaining his agility in the chaos. As he did so, he started to increase his own performance.

Ongoing improvement, *how you make yourself better*, became the last and arguably the biggest difference-maker for thriving in the complex and chaotic storm. With the what, how, who, and when of selling all covered, the time for Brian's ongoing improvement of his proficiency with the anchor points became possible. "What if?" was now a legitimate discussion instead of a subject for cranky salespeople over an after-hours beer.

Face it. Many of you reading this right now need a mirror moment. Read the very next questions slowly.

MIRROR MOMENT

Are you too busy working in your business to work on your business? In other words, when was the last time you actually took a fair and honest assessment of your selling anchor points?

Perhaps reading this book is your way of keeping your skills sharp (and, let's be honest, we're happy you did that). But if your fundamentals, processes, relationships (including the in-house ones), and technology are not securely in place, are you sure that you are actually improving? We want you to be a sales veteran with twenty years of experience, not a sales veteran with one year of experience twenty times.

BUILDING ON THE FOUNDATION

Continuous Improvement

Continuous improvement is a fundamental philosophy of the Total Quality Management movement from the 1980s. Continuous improvement is an ongoing and repeatable process of diagnosing performance gaps with the intention of learning new and creative ways to close them.

CONTINUOUS IMPROVEMENT

Despite the myriad forces of change that were constantly feeding the chaos storm, Brian knew that his business relied on how well he understood and consulted with his buyers. His biggest competitive advantage was his competence in understanding what buyers needed so he could help design, and even deliver, the solutions they wanted. He needed to build and renew customer relationships that delivered ongoing value. This approach was difficult to consistently implement in a chaotic sales environment, but success did come, as he understood what it meant to continuously improve. He literally needed to become agile in the chaos. Because buyers were increasingly demanding unique answers to their unique problems, Brian was forced to constantly acquire deeper understanding and more advanced knowledge, skills, and abilities. He realized that if he wasn't challenging his own thinking, he was running the risk of becoming obsolete.

Pause. Want to test whether you are at risk of becoming obsolete? Look at yourself and where you were as a sales professional three years ago. You should even look at how well you leverage the four anchor points. How embarrassed are you? If you do not see areas that you are genuinely relieved are no longer a point of borderline embarrassment to you, you have a problem. And if that does describe you, don't tell us you have "arrived." We'll ask your customers what they think. Wait. We've already been doing that. That's why we had to write this book.

Are we connecting with you yet? We hope so, because if you cannot secure your anchor points and establish your agility, you (and possibly your whole organization) are probably going under in a chaotic storm. And that's a tragedy we all want to avoid.

Making It Stick

Are your anchors in place? Each anchor builds on the previous one, so you cannot progress from one anchor "level" to the next unless you can answer "agree" to at least three out of four of the statements for each level.

Answer "agree" or "disagree" to each of the following statements.

Anchor 1: Fundamentals

1. I can recite my growth/revenue goals for this year and quarter. _____

2. I don't need to correct my marketing materials in order to be more relevant to customers. _____

3. My first priority is on improving my selling knowledge and skill, and then on managing my results. _____

4. My role is defined by customer need and not internal complexity. _____

Anchor 2: Processes

1. I follow consistent and repeatable processes in selling to and maintaining accounts. _____

2. Discussions about customer needs are more frequent than discussions about the features of products or services. _____

3. I don't have to re-do my own work because I did it right the first time. _____

4. I don't just measure results; I measure the activities that drive those results. _____

Anchor 3: Relationships

1. I consistently give my key customers more attention than every other customer. _____

2. I can name my company's top ten customers. _____

3. I use internal meetings to gain more understanding of my customers more often than troubleshooting "back office" or delivery issues. _____

4. I am held accountable for customer satisfaction, not just revenue targets. _____

Anchor 4: Technology

1. I consistently use technology to help me find important data and information. _____

2. My customer data includes customer interactions, critical account knowledge, and core opportunities.

_____

3. Technology helps my company take care of my customers even when I am not available. _____

4. Technology helps me collaborate and communicate with others in order to keep myself informed about relevant account information. _____

CHAPTER 4

Fundamentals of Sales Chaos: Snowflakes

"No Chaos, No Creation."

Mason Cooley

INTRODUCTION

"Go create some value!" Sarah's sales manager said. "Great, create value, like it's as simple as following a dessert recipe," she thought.

If you sell, you're probably like Sarah in that you must create value with your customer. If you don't, you'll end up in another job. But what is "value" exactly? And how do you "create" value? Lucky for you, understanding Sales Chaos will help you with the most critical aspect of creating value. We call it *recognizing* value. We're not talking about the traditional definition of value you read about or receive in sales training either. When it comes to recognizing value in today's world, you need to approach the concept differently. We know, we know, you're thinking "What do they mean?"

RECOGNIZING VALUE IN THE CHAOS

The best way to help you understand what we're talking about (leveraging Sales Chaos to help you recognize value) is to start with snowflakes. That's right, snowflakes. You know, the white stuff that comes from the sky?

CONSIDER THIS

Evolution of Value

We've been in sales for a long time. We have years of practical experience, and we have also studied professional selling at the academic level. One concept is universal across all our experience – the concept of value. The concept goes way back. When it comes to value, it's important to remember that value is defined *by the customer*, not by you as a salesperson. If the customer defines value differently than you do, he or she will approach the conversation with that definition in mind. And when it comes to defining value, customers have changed dramatically over time, haven't they?

Think about it. Once upon a time:

- Salespeople had to *communicate* value.
- As buyers became more sophisticated, salespeople needed to *create* value.
- After that, buyers evolved again, and salespeople needed to *co-create* value in a meaningful way

- And now salespeople need to *justify* the value they create because the buyer is in complete control

Let us explain.

One of us (Tim) grew up in Hawaii. There's not a lot of snow there (unless you count the month of stuff on the upper slopes of the Big Island). So you can imagine what Tim's first experience trying to snow ski was like.

Fifteen minutes of "lessons" from a friend; then it was off to the ski lift. The sheer terror of trying to time his entry onto the chair (wait a minute – the thing doesn't stop for you to get on?!) was quickly overcome by the beauty of the landscape that unfolded below him. Everything, from stone to tree, was covered in glistening white. The thought then occurred to Tim that all that whiteness was made up of billions and billions of snowflakes. And every one of them was one of a kind.

Have you ever wondered how snowflakes can all be unique? There have been literally countless snowflakes, and yet not one of them has been identical to another. That's really amazing. How does that work? Lucky for you, chaos theory explains it – and explains how to recognize value.

INTRODUCTION TO SNOWFLAKES

One of the cooler bits to understanding chaos theory is the idea of *fractals*. What's a fractal? We're glad you asked. The best way is to show you. Take a look at what happens when we take

BUILDING ON THE FOUNDATION

Fractals

A fractal is an object or quantity that displays self-similarity, in a somewhat technical sense, on all scales. The object need not exhibit exactly the same structure at all scales, but the same "type" of structures must appear on all scales.

Source: http://mathworld.wolfram.com/Fractal.html

a series of shapes and repeat them over and over again. Each shape in the graphic below creates something much more complex by simply repeating itself. Fractal mathematics describes how a shape can be subdivided over and over again, even in a seemingly random order. Clouds, ferns, tree bark—all of these are examples of fractals in the world around us. If you look carefully at the first couple of rows in the graphic, you can tell snowflakes are fractals too.

Let's go a step further. In order for snowflakes to form, tiny particles of dust must be carried up into the atmosphere, where they get covered in ice crystals—typically anywhere from two to two hundred. (Never thought of dirt as a requirement for snow, did you?) Depending on the temperature of the air, these icy dust particles transform into various forms (spikes, prisms, plates, and lacy stars). And now fractal mathematics takes over. As the particles move up and down inside a cloud, each ice crystal clumps together with other ice crystals, randomly repeating the same basic pattern over and over again, until they are heavy enough to tumble down to the earth. Depending on whether or not they fell spinning like a top or tumbled down sideways, they will have either scissor-cut symmetry or lop-sided lumps, each one a never-before-seen creation.

Pause. Did you just see the three elements required to shape snowflakes? There's temperature, the number of other ice crystals in the air (determined by humidity), and the direction they fell to the earth (determined by air currents). We point out these factors because it really only takes three things to create infinite possibilities.

We'll say it again: Infinite possibilities come from a limited set of factors.

Sounds a lot like working with customers, doesn't it?

CUSTOMERS ARE LIKE SNOWFLAKES

Have you ever learned something new in a sales meeting? Have you ever been surprised by new players? Has the deal you thought you were going to sell changed dramatically, to the point at which you sold something completely different? If you've been selling for any length of time, you have probably noticed that, even if the conversation is repeated the next week with the same people, the results can be wildly different each time.

We call this *"watching a snowflake form."* It describes exactly how customers buy. Let's face it. The purpose of your business is to create and keep customers. Ideally, you want to do that in the easiest, simplest way. But each one of your customers is unique, just like snowflakes. In a single deal, you have fractals all over the place. Start with multiple opportunities to address — and just as likely, multiple decision-makers. These two factors alone can create a one-of-a-kind snowstorm. Add in your own company's ability to respond to opportunities and the decision-makers back at your own home office and you, dear friend, had better be equipped for a blizzard.

What if you could actually recognize how each snowflake is developing and even slow down the flurry of action around you? What if you could turn infinite possibilities into another core advantage? Think this kind of snow mastery is a "Matrix"-like illusion? Think again.

Sales Chaos Theory says that when you understand how your customer's definition of value forms, you are on the path of truly recognizing value. Once you recognize the value that the customer is looking for, you can begin to harness the chaos around you so your sales conversations become more relevant to buyers.

THE FULL VALUE EXPERIENCE–
UNDERSTANDING EACH SNOWFLAKE

When we began to look at how customers buy, we wanted to identify the essential factors that make up the broader customer experience. That is when it hit us. *The customer is defining the overall experience of value, not the transaction.*

Think about it. How does the customer define value? Well, if you recall, we said in Chapter 1 that "Full Value" is basically anything that a customer can complain about. That is too simple a definition. We will get into the grittier details in another chapter, but we want you consider full value as the entire bundle of needs that drive the buyer. It is bigger than just the product or service you sell, which is why we use complaints as the easiest way to introduce the concept.

Now take that thought and apply it to the overall buying experience. If full value is the "what" your customers buy, the overall experience is the "how." The full value experience has three components:

- Discovering value,
- Positioning value, and
- Delivering value

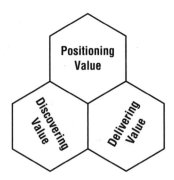

Picture the full value experience as being made up of three essential elements or ice crystals. (Remember, we're talking about snowflakes here!) Each crystal fits together in a unique way. At the surface, these three crystals represent the components necessary for you to create the full value experience with your buyer, just as every snowflake is made of ice crystals formed on a piece of dust, except that in the full value experience, the piece of dust is the value the customer is trying to define. In the simplest possible terms, this value can be *anything your customer can complain about*. And how those complaints are handled (positively or negatively) will define the shape of each crystal. Obviously, the concept of value is much more than a laundry list of customer complaints, but you get the idea, right?

Let's take a moment to calibrate and define these three components, shown in the graphic.

Element 1: Discovering Value

The first element, Discovering Value, is about helping your customer articulate his or her need(s), understand alternatives, and see obstacles. It's about defining the chaos in a way that separates what is happening now from what should be going on. As a sales professional, you are actually responsible for helping the buyer achieve this clarity and, if you are able, for helping the buyer prioritize the alternatives and determine what success should look like. When this is done properly, the customer has discovered the value he or she is looking for. The bottom line: *The customer agrees on what value is needed.*

Element 2: Positioning Value

The next element, Positioning Value, is about helping your customer define what the best deal looks like. It's about you taking the vague sense of success that the buyer has pictured in his or her mind and transforming it into a legitimate and quantifiable solution. You may have to go through the process of negotiating this offer (and you may not). When you position value properly, the customer can act upon it. The bottom line: *The customer agrees on what value he or she can have.*

Element 3: Delivering Value

The third element, Delivering Value, is about helping your customer to not only achieve the success he or she pictured, but to leverage it. Protect the value the customer bought and make sure that the credit goes to whomever it should go. Look for other alternatives that can increase the value that was bought. Identify what worked so it can be repeated. Identify what did not so it can be avoided. When value is delivered right, the value the customer has paid for is being delivered. The bottom line: *The customer agrees on the impact of the value provided.*

Every full value experience has these three elements, even if you don't work with all of them. This concept is massive. If the full value experience is made up of these three crystals, you don't have to push the sales conversation into a mass-production mold. In fact, you can allow the conversation to go wherever the customer wants it to go, knowing that it will never drift outside of these three topics. Knowing the conversation stays within the boundaries of discovering, positioning, and delivering value, you can watch the snowflake form without getting lost in the process. This is the secret of recognizing value.

And value really is what drives customer behavior: three ice crystals, all built from the requirements of the full value experience, driving infinite possibilities. How does this impact you? The biggest impact is that the traditional sales process has devolved into chaos. If you are expecting your customers to move in a traditional pattern, how are you going to respond if they suddenly loop back or lurch ahead? Well, how fast do you want the snowflakes to move?

WHY THE TRADITIONAL SALES PROCESS DOESN'T WORK

Unfortunately, most sales process definitions are written from the perspective of the seller. Or worse, by someone with a background in finance or marketing (sorry we couldn't resist). Remember the three forces constantly at work in Sales Chaos: the non-linear, full value, and community? Think about what those forces do to the thought processes of buyers. You find non-linear definitions of value that can shift depending on which member of the community you are talking with. If you put yourself into the shoes of a buyer, you quickly realize that you could demand any or all three value requirements at any given moment. The traditional sales process cannot handle that.

But if you can shift your activity to calibrate against how your customers are creating snowflakes–we mean identifying needs and then making buying decisions–you can literally shape your customer conversations and stand above your competition. You no longer need a traditional selling process. Instead, you have a "capturing full value" experience that your customers will be much happier to participate in. At the very least, you can decipher what the customer is saying and how you should best respond.

What is most important about this view of how selling and buying interact is that it is *non-linear*. Full value, even when it is created in a non-sequential way, will still make complete sense when you see the final picture (much like the beauty of a snowflake when it is fully formed). This is a vital point. By definition, a linear view of reality means that $A + B = C$. In chaos, $A + B = A$, wait . . . purple, then A. Where the heck did C go? Oh yeah, it's sitting on someone's wall as a motivational poster.

PAY ATTENTION

Actions and activities, as well as human behaviors, repeat themselves over time, if you study them long enough.

ORDER FROM THE CHAOS

Just remember that chaos theory allows you to reveal the order in something that appears to be random. Chaos theory is not about managing random complexity, but about looking into the random complexity to find the patterns and the non-chaotic. Hence the intellectual leap to professional selling.

Actions and activities, as well as human behaviors, actually repeat all the time, just not in a precise, linear way. In other words, you can find patterns in the chaos. If you have been in professional selling for any length of time, you probably have come to realize that there are situations, experiences, and activities that seem to repeat themselves like an endless *Groundhog Day* experience. You remember that movie? Bill Murray's character woke up to experience the exact same day over and over again, no matter what happened throughout the day. Even his own death was erased so that he woke up to relive the same day in a kind of endless time warp. Sometimes the day went well. Sometimes the day went horribly wrong. His mission became one of simply accepting the familiar with the unfamiliar, to stop trying to control the moment. Once he realized that he could not control it, he started to learn from and even enjoy it. What a great analogy for approaching your selling career.

EMBRACE THE CHAOS

Pause. Do you enjoy it? Your business, that is. Do you enjoy the business you're in or are you struggling to survive the day? We ask this because, for some of you, you need to realize that the only way to enjoy the chaos is let yourself become part of it, to drift through it, looking for the spots where the chaos creates patterns and starts to make sense. Just like Eric.

Eric is one of the most successful salespeople we know. He's sold for almost twenty years in some of the most competitive and complex environments. While Eric has many unique qualities, it seems that he has an uncanny ability to be at the right place at the right time. Somehow, he is able to find the largest account within the territory (you know, the one that everyone else thought would be a waste of time) or the largest deal in the account (again, the one that nobody else in his sales organization could see coming). While many sales books would have you believe that Eric has the "natural ability" to sell or possesses eternal optimism and drive, from what we can tell, these aren't the definitive contributors to his success. Sure, they help, but Eric has developed the ability to look at his business with soft eyes, to see the patterns overlap in the chaos.

Eric once explained that his approach is not unlike looking at a jigsaw puzzle scattered on the floor. While many people see an impossible task, Eric looks for patterns and creates a mental picture while everyone else is finding the first corner pieces.

"Somehow, I can see the picture in my mind, even though the pieces aren't connected," said Eric. "I can group the puzzle pieces by color and connect them into some sort of mental picture while cross-referencing that mental picture with what I know to be true. It has to be a picture of something or someone!"

While Eric would argue this is a sign of pure genius (just ask him!), we would argue that he has snowflakes nailed. Hc can see the ice crystals forming chaos snowflakes in the air.

The key to Eric's ability is that he isn't trying to force an image into his mind. He is letting the puzzle pieces provide just enough data that Point X and Point Y can sit right next to each other without screwing up the final image. In other words, he is not trying to force the final deal to look like a preconceived image. In this same way, you may need to develop the ability to let one part of the sales experience sit directly next to (and perhaps on top of) another part of the sales experience without a predetermined picture in your mind. Quit trying to force the sales process into a linear, time-sensitive pattern. Use the time that you would normally take to find the puzzle corners and start working on recognizing the picture of what your value will look like.

HELLO, NON-LINEAR CUSTOMER!

Since we're talking about snowflakes and how they're all unique (yet built the same), perhaps it is best if we take another look at someone else who is vital to this discussion: the customer. In our research for this book, we discovered a consistent theme. Each customer has his or her own unique puzzle called "what customers want." And what customers want is best described as "rigid flexibility." We mean rigid enough to be trustworthy and flexible enough to be helpful. In the most amazing twist of this story, we've discovered that your customers don't want you to be linear. They want you to be agile, chaos snowflake masters. They want you to help them see the snowflakes as they form so that they are not overwhelmed by the snowflakes they create.

Pause. Hear one thing. DO NOT think of the full value experience as a modified version of beginning, middle, and end. It is not a linear buying process. DO think of it as three ice crystals that have formed together to make a unified whole, as three areas where the buyer could take you at any given moment. Every buying decision has all three components, just as every snowflake is made of ice crystals formed on a piece of dust under the right conditions. However, you can literally be brought into the conversation with a customer at any point in the full value experience. It is, and always will be, a non-linear chaos pattern.

Imagine that you are a buyer. You may want to bring up delivering value in the beginning. The last vendor may have screwed up so badly after making a bunch of empty promises about delivering value that you want to talk about it up-front. Likewise, you may want to talk about discovering value in the middle of the experience, as a new opportunity is uncovered during negotiations. And just because you didn't define it before the sales rep started into his final pitch doesn't mean that you don't want to address it now. Heck, as a buyer, you're even willing to pay for it.

But if you try to keep everything defined in terms of beginning, middle, and end and organized into neat little swim lanes for every transaction, you will only become confused and fatigued. So quit wasting your energy on keeping the experience defined in lines. Your business does not rely on that kind of simple sales deals anyway. The most significant and rewarding deals, the ones that actually keep your business afloat in the chaos, are the most complex. You would never try to shove some inadequate definition of the beginning, middle, and end onto a huge deal so that you could force it into a transactional sales process. You have more important things to figure out, like your strategy for discovering what your customers really want, persuading them to agree on the solution you are prepared to develop, and making sure that your own company will deliver the full value you promised. You will likely work on all three components of full value at the same time.

We recognize that most people want a beginning, a middle, and an end in their sales processes. But remember that most complex sales experiences are simply not linear. If there were just one decision-maker, if the buyer didn't have access to your data, if just dumping more potential leads into your sales funnel actually worked.... If, if, if. Dream on. Those days are long gone. The conversation will go all over the place, and the opportunity will at times seem lost, but the final offering you will give to your customer will actually make sense. So face it, the only thing linear about your business today is your calendar, and the sooner we can all agree on this the better.

SHIFT YOUR THINKING: FROM PROCESS TO EXPERIENCE

Fundamentally, it's about shifting the way you think. We know that some of you are still struggling with this force called the non-linear. Here's a tip. *Stop focusing on your sales process.* Just let it go from your mind. Right now. *Start focusing on your customer's buying experience.* Shift your thinking to the moment you are in, even as it is happening. The impact of this mental adjustment is amazing.

You will find that, instead of trying to rush through the PowerPoint slides you prepared for the meeting, you will read and react to the chaos that your customers are swirling in with the kind of grounded security they wish they had. You will adapt. You will be supportive. You will focus on the full value that your customer wants you to capture in that moment. You will follow through on your promises. In other words, *you will be rigid enough to be trustworthy and flexible enough to be helpful.*

AN EXAMPLE OF THE FULL-VALUE EXPERIENCE

For an example of a company that has made this shift, look at Apple. Apple stores have done a great job of creating the full value experience. When you walk into one of their locations, the layout is a little confusing. Where are the aisles? Where are the hanging signs? Instead, you find a pleasant enough individual asking, "How can I help you?" Based on your answer, you are sent to either discover value, position value, or deliver value. There is no immediate launch into the daily specials, no attempt to get you to start at one section and move to the next, just a polite set of instructions on how to achieve what you are looking for. And, by the way, while you are in the discover/position/deliver part of the store, feel free to drift around and experience the other aspects of value. Need to have your iPod checked at the Genius

Bar (delivering value), then talk to a salesperson about some new apps you can download (positioning value) while your friend looks at the new MacBooks (discovering value). It is all located in one, open room. When you look at their growing success in this way—as a non-linear, full value, community-based model built to fulfill the buyer's expectations—it's easy to compare Apple to others and see why their biggest competitors keep trying to reinvent themselves. Oops. Did we just say that out loud?

But the larger question looms above us: If this is how people want to buy, why don't we all sell that way?

Instead of trying to force every opportunity or every decision-maker into one phase of your selling process (like closing), here is your chance to be rigidly flexible. If you are genuinely prepared to enter the chaos, simply identify what value requirement your customer is talking about and respond accordingly. This is the essence of recognizing and creating full value.

Make sense? Great.

A QUICK TEST: RECOGNIZING FULL VALUE

We have a quick test for you.

Jose the buyer is ready to sign a new contract. Everything is ready to go when he asks you about your customer service processes. Pause. What aspect of the full value experience do you recognize? What's the meaning behind his question?

Pause. Before you go on, read this mirror moment.

> ### MIRROR MOMENT
>
> Do you even stop the conversation at times like these to probe for clarity or do you just tell people like Jose about how your customer service does a great job at delivering value and push him toward the close? Want to really poke a soft spot? Tell us about the last time you paused and asked for clarity. Can you think of a time? Some of you reading this are hearing crickets right now.

Back to Jose. Upon asking him the requisite "Why do you ask?" you discover that his company is struggling to track purchases with their new inventory management system. Some "intelligent" person at his corporate headquarters has derailed the entire purchasing process and Jose is looking for someone to help him solve a problem. Sounds like an opportunity to discover value, not deliver it. Shucks, you may even be able to define a measurable solution to position value with your agreed-on offering and strengthen the deal. Plus, you set yourself up to successfully deliver value now, because Jose is ready to focus on the original deal. You are recognizing the customer's entire definition of full value. And you are using your understanding of the experience to create full value. You just slowed down a bunch of snowflakes.

Congratulations, you just took your first step to harnessing the chaos.

Making It Stick

Identify who is involved within your organization as well as the buyer organization as you have sales conversations across the three phases of the full value experience. Also identify what resources you need to make each phase successful.

Phase 1: Discovering Value
- Who is involved?

- What resources are needed?

Phase 2: Positioning Value
- Who is involved?

- What resources are needed?

Phase 3: Delivering Value

- Who is involved?

- What resources are needed?

C H A P T E R

A Recap of Thinking Differently

"Chaos is a friend of mine."

Bob Dylan

THIS CHAPTER PROVIDES YOU A REVIEW OF WHAT WE have covered thus far. Our goal is to make sure you understand the foundation of Sales Chaos so that you can begin thinking differently and change the relevance of your conversations with buyers. This new way of thinking is critical before moving into the next section on selling differently.

REVIEW: SALES CHAOS

How are you doing with the concept of Sales Chaos? As you can tell from the material in the last four chapters, the phrase "Sales Chaos" actually has nothing to do with whether or not the sales experience is wildly out of control. Quite the contrary, Sales Chaos is actually about identifying patterns that will make the sales experience smoother than what you are experiencing now. Just to be clear, we're not saying that salespeople should just engage in selling without being prepared. That would be unprofessional. Worse, being unprepared will actually contribute to the chaos by introducing new butterflies. We're quite sure your customers wouldn't tolerate salespeople who contribute to the chaos. And since we've used these principles to grow our own business in a down economy and land a ton of revenue for our own companies (as well as for our customers), we're quite confident this approach to selling still appears smooth, ordered, and organized to our customers and clients.

If we could simplify the entire Sales Chaos message for you, it would be that your business reality may appear to be completely random and chaotic, but patterns and order can be found and harnessed in order to have more relevant sales conversations with buyers. Many salespeople we talk to seem to think that today's business reality has become too complicated to manage, but that's a cop-out. It's just not true. While the selling system is complex, individual salespeople can find a way to handle the complexity and have meaningful sales conversations with their buyers. In fact, in the first four chapters, we gave you what you needed to begin choosing the right daily activities and help you slow down the chaos so you begin having those meaningful conversations. We provided a framework to help you understand what it takes to have those meaningful conversations. That same framework can help you slow down the random complexity of your day-to-day work, based on your new understanding of Sales Chaos. This will help you stay ahead of your customers and competition and achieve long-term, sustainable success, one sales conversation at a time.

CONSIDER THIS

Have you ever wondered why things randomly happen in business? Or have you ever been surprised by an unexpected outcome? It's just Sales Chaos in action.

REVIEW: COMPLEXITY

We've also given you what you need to understand the complexity of the business market while maintaining order and effectiveness. As any savvy businessperson can tell you, driving revenue requires an integrated approach to selling, marketing, servicing, supply chain, etc. As you have already discovered, whenever the customer is involved, random complexity reigns. And it's not just random complexity at the organizational level, but random complexity at the personal level. How can something that is random also be ordered at the same time? That's where all the science came into the discussion.

When we introduced Sales Chaos (and chaos theory in general), you discovered that chaos can actually explain things that are extremely complex. For example, look outside your window right now. Think about what it takes to explain the weather happening at this moment. Better yet, think about what it takes to forecast the weather that will happen next week.

CONSIDER THIS

Randomness reigns in weather patterns like temperature, humidity, wind conditions, and barometric pressure. The same can be said for business markets and economics.

Many complex factors intermingle to produce a weather system that is constantly in motion. They include heat, cold, wind, and humidity. Unless you are God, every attempt you make to organize and re-create order will be smacked around by the law of nature that says unexpected changes will occur when these forces collide. What we're talking about doesn't just apply to weather patterns. Think about changes in the stock market or even the simple swinging of a pendulum as some of the ways that chaos can be found around us.

Going a step further, we're willing to bet that chaos explains a lot about your business. Just as modern business evolved from the "every price is negotiable" haggling at the local market to become the complete acceptance of sticker price at the local shopping mall, professional business is becoming something else. Being less mechanical in this new business reality will actually make you far more agile in your response to the chaos. You will see patterns emerge out of the random complexity, and you will even open up the possibility of harnessing the chaos.

As you probably have guessed, harnessing chaos is not an easy thing. It requires that you do two things. First, you must have the ability to get inside the chaos and not be intimidated by it. Second, you must have the ability to slow it down so that you can make the right decisions. For both of these reasons, you learned about butterflies, anchor points, and snowflakes.

REVIEW: BUTTERFLIES

Keeping your eyes open for butterflies means that you are putting your influence into the actions that lead to the right results, and not just into the results themselves. You cannot "do" a result. You do the things that lead to results. If you do not recognize that even the most minor fluctuation can create massive impact later on, you will constantly be battered by the chaos. Just remember that you cannot see every single butterfly. You can only anticipate where they may appear (PTER) and maintain a state of professionalism and readiness. Understand that the chaos will not go away, but you will know where to put your influence to slow it down enough to catch your breath—and perhaps even surge ahead of your competition.

REVIEW: ANCHOR POINTS

Knowing about anchor points means that you can create a foundation for your personal agility within the chaos. By securing your fundamentals, processes, relationships, and technology, you will stop being thrown around and constantly reacting to the things happening around you. As a result, you will acquire the most precious of selling resources: time. Again, the chaos will not go away, but you will have enough stability to start thinking about what could be done to improve performance and to strengthen your business in a way that balances the strategic against the tactical and the proactive against the reactive.

REVIEW: SNOWFLAKES

Understanding how snowflakes form means that you will keep discussions (both externally and internally) focused on the full value your customers are trying to experience. By keeping your focus, you will soon develop the ability to guide how snowflakes develop without crushing their uniqueness. And most importantly, your customers will be able to experience the full value they are looking for, even if they don't know what they want at first.

That's it. Taken together, your understanding of butterflies, anchor points, and snowflakes will simplify your approach to selling and prepare you to harness the chaos. Sounds fun, doesn't it?

But before we explain how you can leverage Sales Chaos to succeed, we offer a word of caution.

WHICH WAY WILL YOU GO?

In our experience of teaching Sales Chaos Theory, we've found that the revelation of what it really takes to succeed in selling in today's business reality creates a decision point for salespeople. Just like the choice between the red and blue pills Morpheus offered in the movie *The Matrix*, salespeople have to make a choice. As we said earlier, the first is *rejecting the newly defined reality.* By this decision, salespeople simply choose to ignore what we have taught them about Sales Chaos. They attempt to rationalize their own comfort levels and their own understanding of what it takes to succeed in professional selling today. Accepting chaos in business is simply too crazy to them.

> ### PAY ATTENTION
> You have a choice to make. Reject the new reality or embrace it.

The second possible decision is *embracing the newly defined reality.* With this outcome, salespeople embrace what they already suspect – that patterns and order can be found within the chaos, just not in the way that they expected. Embracing the new reality requires salespeople to make a conscious choice to see the world of business differently and relearn everything they thought they knew. Embracing the newly defined reality also requires a willingness (and even an openness) to accept the possibility of new outcomes, actions, and results.

This choice is illustrated by a conversation Tim once had with a savvy sales manager in South Africa regarding the concept of Sales Chaos. After hearing about butterflies/anchor points/snowflakes and how they impact the day-to-day lives of today's salespeople, the sales manager didn't run away but ran toward the new selling reality. He said, "I totally understand what you're saying, and it does sound like the world I live in, but how can I learn more about what you have just taught me? And more importantly, how can I use this concept to actually drive more sales?" As he confronted reality, this sales manager started by choosing the right outcome, which positioned him to begin the journey toward selling differently.

Are you willing to embrace this newly defined reality? Are you comfortable with all of this talk about butterflies, anchor points, and snowflakes? Are you willing to accept that you have changes to make and that, by making them, you will achieve different (and better) business results? It means that you will think differently. It means that people will actually hear you talking about Sales Chaos. And it means that you will get strange looks, even while you are cashing checks.

If you cannot embrace these changes, put the book down. Now. The message isn't going to be much better as you read on. Even if you apply what we're about to teach, you are going to get frustrated, confused, and a bit angry because the world of business still won't work the way it is "supposed" to. Seriously, we cannot help you with that.

If, on the other hand, you are willing (and dare we say eager?) about making changes that drive a whole new way of thinking, keep reading. Start looking at yourself even more critically. Accept our sarcastic pokes and prods as necessary to the learning process. We do not need you to prove anything to us. We need you to prove it to yourself.

So come along. Let's get agile.

Making It Stick

Slowing Down the Chaos – Creating a Journal Entry

Take a moment and reflect on what we have been saying. We have used a lot of stories and examples while also relaying a lot of information about Sales Chaos Theory. Before moving on to the next chapter, take a moment to reflect.

Using the space provided, write some notes to yourself below.

1. What are your key takeaways from Chapters 1 through 4?

2. Have you identified any areas that you personally want to improve upon?

3. Is there someone you know you can discuss this with?

4. In the next ninety days, what are the top two or three priorities you want to put into action?

Send us your thoughts!

Email for Brian: Brian@SaleChaos.com
Email for Tim: Tim@SalesChaos.com

SECTION
2

Selling Differently, Part One

The Agility Selling Methodology

"Chaos is the score upon which reality is written."

Henry Miller

INTRODUCTION

Throughout the book, we have made comments about being agile. So far, we have talked about communicating relevance to buyers so you become more *agile* in meeting customer demands. We have called for *agile* sales processes, *agile* responses to market conditions, and *agile* hiring processes. All of this agility can create momentum through more relevance for any business. And that's what's needed when it comes to addressing chaos.

So before we get too far into this chapter, let's ask a quick question. Are you an agile seller? Actually, forget that. A better question is this: Would your customers say that you are an agile seller?

While you may be quick to answer, think about being agile as defined by the Oxford English dictionary:

1. Characterized by quickness, lightness, and ease of movement; nimble.
2. Mentally quick or alert,

While many salespeople would readily say they are agile, they can't necessarily explain what they actually did to become agile in the first place. Most will agree that bringing agility to sales is important, but not be able to explain how to do it.

> ## PAY ATTENTION
>
> We're going to go out on a limb and say it: You don't know your customers as well as you think you do. Spend more time studying them. Take more time to understand the pressures they face, what trends are influencing them, and what challenges will create problems for them.

THE CHALLENGE

In our work over the last decade, we interviewed and labored alongside sales professionals from a variety of industries, geographies, and regions of the world. The single biggest complaint we heard over and over again was a lack of execution around responding to customers.

We first started hearing that salespeople didn't think they were getting the support they needed. Then we began hearing that individual teams within marketing and sales weren't supportive of the selling effort. To be candid, even with this information staring us in the face, we thought salespeople were just being overly cynical. But when we started researching the perceptions of buyers themselves, we discovered the salespeople were correct—even customers and buyers didn't think sales organizations knew them well enough! In fact, customers thought salespeople didn't understand the problems they faced, the market conditions impacting their jobs, or the way they made decisions.

Did you catch that subtle shift? The customer turned the conversation from frustration with the sales organization to frustration with the individual salesperson. Surely, they're not talking about you, right?

MIRROR MOMENT

Here's a mirror moment. If we asked your customers to assess whether or not you know them well enough, what would they tell us? Now ask yourself this: Do you consistently create and chase tornadoes, fumble around your anchor points, or get smothered by snowflakes?

If you answered yes to any of these, you are just as guilty as your organization. And you probably don't know your customers as well as you think you do. You can change, and it all begins with thinking differently. But thinking differently is just the first step. You must now sell differently, and that is easier said than done.

THE EVOLUTION OF PROFESSIONAL SELLING

It's time for another history lesson. Do you know the origin of sales? We mean the first transaction exchanging money for a good or service. In academic circles, the most common answer is the one you may be thinking right now: prostitution. Yep. The world's oldest profession is likely the great, great-grandma no one in sales wants to talk about. Sadly, many people outside of sales still equate the modern profession of selling with prostitution. Used car salesman, anyone?

The impact is that both buyer and seller can become conditioned to the less than ethical practices that this mental model evokes. Just look at the list of words associated with the word "seller" from thesaurus.com: hawker, huckster, peddler, pitchperson, and rep. They don't make your buttons burst with pride, do they?

But can we blame the people who keep those terms alive? There are far too many stories of salespeople still operating as if they are working a street corner. It makes you wish that salespeople listened to the Quakers more.

What? Quakers? Yes, most definitely the Quakers. Think dark clothing, wide-brimmed hats, and oatmeal. In the 1700s, the

Quakers were barred from universities, which thrust the Quakers into the trading business. The result? A massive change in how sales were done. Instead of bartering and bickering over prices at the local market, Quakers set the most honest price they could. They took the principle of integrity to other parts of business as well. It worked so well that customers flocked to it in masses. In fact, many people were drawn to imitate the Quaker business model just to stay alive. The result was a transformation into a business model that we try to follow today.

If you add in the Industrial Revolution, you can really see how modern selling evolved. Science, education, and commerce all converged when the mechanical took over. People found all kinds of ways to improve and streamline the way people learned and worked, especially when the chance to make a few more dollars was introduced. Process became king, and that thinking hit a high note in sales when Joseph Juran (the 80/20 guy) declared, "There should be no reason our familiar principles of quality and process engineering would not work in the sales process."

This means that if you try to be an ethical, process-driven salesperson, you probably think of yourself as a true sales professional. But we don't think you can use this definition any more. In fact, if you use just these two criteria, you aren't a sales professional. You are a sales dinosaur.

We know what some of you are thinking. Just hear us out. We do not want to weaken the need for business ethics in any way. If anything, ethics should be amplified for today's reality. But when it comes to being driven by the sales process, we want to attack it with both hands.

For more than one hundred years, the profession of selling has been enamored with the sales process. The National Cash Register Company (NCR) is credited as the originator of modern selling. In 1893, John Henry Patterson started the first sales training school built on principles his brother-in-law developed. We basically call this model *transactional selling* today. The beauty of transactional selling is that it made the transaction repeatable. This was revolutionary. A salesperson could actually follow steps and experience a certain percentage of success, depending on his or her ability to follow that process over and over again. And the numbers game in sales was thus born.

Somewhere in the mid-1900s, IBM started playing with a sales process that we now call *solution selling*. Not to be confused with the branded work of Michael Bosworth, the core idea of this process was to bundle products and services to obtain a larger sale. Solution selling created a new level of complexity, as customer offerings were now being built to fit with each other instead of just sitting on the order sheet as an endless list of items for sale. Cross-selling and up-selling were now a permanent part of the chaos.

Then, largely due to the work of people like Mack Hanan, Neil Rackham, and others, the idea of *consultative selling* took off in 1970s and 1980s. This robust process actually identified and solved the customer problem at a higher price point and grabbed all kinds of attention. Selling the same stuff for more money? What a great concept. But it also increased the level of complexity in selling because the salesperson was trying to solve bigger problems. Which led to more non-salespeople involved in the customer experience. Oh joy.

Fast-forward to the late 1980s and 1990s, where you will find the idea of *strategic selling* growing to dominate the current thinking. This process, largely credited to Robert Miller and Stephen Heiman, does a fantastic job of mapping the complexity of the customer relationship to see opportunities. The clarity and insight this process produces is very useful, but–um–we have a problem here. The greater the complexity, the more time it takes to map. And the map is only good for a limited amount of time. This is not exactly a process that the vast majority of salespeople can use, since time is almost more precious than air.

So why the extended history lesson? Simple. We have now reached a point in the profession of selling that requires change. To be specific, all of the methodologies we described above (and even the stuff from a host of really powerful contributors we didn't quote) all rely on *process*.

But the question remains: If we are going to embrace today's reality, why don't these process-driven approaches work like they used to? How can linear thinking accurately navigate the complexity of how customers buy? Of course, linear thinking can organize the steps and activity, but can linear thinking help you solve customer problems?

Let's face it. The sales process is simply too confining and restrained. Isolated by itself, it doesn't help you address all of the buyer's core needs that define full value any more. If you live by process, you will die by process. Sure, you could argue that these processes tried to keep up with each successive shift in complexity, but there comes a point when the idea that you can keep the forces of chaos contained by sales process becomes outdated—no matter what management wants to believe.

BUILDING ON THE FOUNDATION

Evolution of Selling

Selling has evolved over the years. It's become more specialized than ever before. Think about it. The evolution has occurred from:

- Transactional to solution selling

  And then from

- Solution selling to consultative selling

  And then from

- Consultative selling to strategic selling

  And now

- Strategic selling evolving to??

What About Agility Selling?

All of these selling legacies exist in the most complicated organizations, and that's ok. The goal is to align these selling legacies to how the customer buys. Agility Selling can exist within all of these legacy selling motions as a way to handle complexity.

And now we are back to staring at the swirling cloud of complexity that describes today's business reality. And in this complexity, which we call Sales Chaos, the power of the sales process is no longer what it used to be. Something is missing, and we believe that something should give salespeople the ability to have more valuable discussions, no matter what environment they are working in.

Enter Agility Selling, where instead of process we push *patterns*.

You see, with patterns, you can still operate inside the system of selling with a certain degree of effectiveness. Process exists, but it is no longer the driver. Patterns are. And if you know what patterns to look for, the chaos slows down. People can still exchange value, and businesses can still prepare for this exchange in a way that is both profitable and practical.

The key is that the patterns do not always happen in the same order. Read that again. *Patterns do not always happen in the same order*. This is where the reliance on process breaks down and becomes downright clumsy.

And you know what clumsy sounds like. Perhaps you've heard some of these. "We're like turning a big ship. Nothing happens quickly." Or perhaps, "It takes forever to get anything changed around here." Or maybe you have heard our personal favorite coming from the mouth of one of your customers: "You, I like. It's your company that is driving me crazy."

All of these are indicators that you and your organization are bogged down with too much process. It's time to start making a change, which is why we spent all that time explaining how to think differently in the earlier chapters.

But while we were detailing how to think differently, we were also giving you the patterns that you should be using to sell differently:

- *The Butterfly Effect:* any minor fluctuation can turn into a major disruption later.
- *Anchor Points:* no matter what kind of chaos you work in, there will be points of density that you can tie into and create stability.

- *Snowflakes:* while every customer interaction will be unique, they will all have three essential elements that pull all of the buyer's core needs together and eventually create a full value experience.

You must know these patterns to be able to use them, but you cannot predict the future with them. In other words, the patterns will definitely occur in your business. We just wish that we could predict when that will happen for you (but we can't). A pattern may start at any point in time or in any place during the conversation. A pattern can appear during an external customer conversation or even an internal back-office conversation. A pattern can appear in one customer interaction and not appear in the next.

Look back on the last three months. Did any butterflies, shifting anchor points, or snowflakes appear? Sure they did. But can you tell when they will appear in the next three months? No way. You must know these patterns to be able to use them, but you cannot predict the future with them.

But once you understand the patterns, you can begin to learn from them. You will be able to leverage them to see what you may not have seen before. You will see:

- Personal strengths and weaknesses
- Blind spots you didn't see before
- Organizational constraints and bottlenecks
- Obstacles to information flow
- Critical barriers to communicating value
- Ways to organize information
- Shifts in buyer decision making

And once you start seeing these, you will start getting a sense of what you should be doing. Amazingly, you will find yourself more proactive than you have been in years. And you will not freak out when a pattern disrupts or even disappears because you understand that the pattern is part of your business, not a danger to it. Imagine that.

PAY ATTENTION

Hear us clearly. We are thankful for each of these approaches to sales, as they moved the definition of professional selling forward. We are not discrediting them in any way. Without them, selling would be little more than a glorified carnival job. In fact, there are still situations in which they remain incredibly appropriate.

PATTERN RECOGNITION– THE KEY TO AGILITY

We have found that recognizing patterns is the only way for people to cope, and even harness, the chaos around them. So we developed the idea of Agility Selling as a way to transform pattern recognition into the foundation of knowing how to sell differently.

With Agility Selling, people can study the complexity around them and then deal with the randomness they find. (How's that for a concept?) To be more blunt, Agility Selling isn't about oversimplifying the selling profession but about changing your sales approach in order to see through the random patterns and then adapt to the ever-changing world around you.

The good news is that, once you learn to recognize the patterns in the chaos, you can use the Agility Selling methodology to start selling more effectively. Even though you may experience chaos regularly, you will start adapting and changing your behavior. This change in your approach will separate you from the competition. When you behave differently from the competition, you will differentiate yourself with buyers. But when Agility Selling isn't applied, we have found that salespeople aren't able to cope with (or overcome) the chaos.

Face it. Most people who work in a selling organization are locked (by choice or not) into the daily grind of transactions.

Using Pareto's principle, 80 percent of what someone sees in an average day will be coming from any given company's transactional, less-than-strategic, smaller-revenue-generating customer segment. That's a lot of noise. No wonder folks don't see the need for agility. Being agile in a transactional environment doesn't make sense. Why? For starters, there's not enough time. Secondly, assuming you had the time, would being agile with those kind of limited value opportunities be the best approach? Maybe. But probably not.

But what if you changed your perspective? What if every time you were engaging with that 20 percent of the business that drove greater performance and profits, the kind of success that your customers are proud of you for achieving (because you gave them the value they wanted all along), a bright green light physically appeared in the room?

BUILDING ON THE FOUNDATION

In our first book, *World-Class Selling: New Sales Competencies* (Lambert, Ohai, & Kerkhoff, 2009), we worked with thousands of sales managers, sales trainers, and sales professionals to define the sales profession.

The ramifications of the definition we came up with should not be underestimated. We say that:

1. Selling requires a systems approach to be effective.

2. The focus of the profession is on the human agents involved in the exchange between customer and seller.

3. The purpose of the profession is a financial exchange based on value between the buyer and the seller.

Note: Sales Chaos is primarily about the systems approach required to be effective.

Picture this. A salesperson is sitting in his office and calls a customer. In fact, that salesperson has been making phone calls all day. Call after call after call. Suddenly, on this particular call, that bright green light turns on overhead. Remember, the light signifies the need to be agile, to turn on one's mind and look for patterns in the chaos. That salesperson is now acutely aware that every word, every thought, is to be intentional. What would change from the way he had been acting during his previous calls? That salesperson would purposely slow down and think through every action. He would become keenly aware that, at this particular moment in time, he has the potential to not just communicate value, but to create it.

Now imagine what it would be like if the phone call (or email or customer visit) occurred at the main office and everyone—*every*one—could see the light go on that reminds them to be agile. What would change in those people's behavior? More importantly, what impact would this have on the customer?

CHANGING YOUR APPROACH

We think it would be bigger than just changing how salespeople sell. We think that the organization would start to change. The metrics would change. How bonuses are determined would change. The leadership would change. The entire operating philosophy would change. Agility would become something that is bigger than a sales process. It would become a cultural value, a cornerstone of both strategy and operations. With the customer at the center of things, salespeople would be able to bridge the chasm between the people within their own organization and the buyers within the customer's organization with greater agility. Wouldn't that be nice?

Where were we? Oh yeah. Setting you up for a mirror moment.

In order to be agile, you have more choices to make. Each of these choices will directly impact your ability to do more than understand what is happening around you. Make the wrong choice, and you will not only be swept away by the chaos (yet again), but you would have the added benefit of explicitly, painfully, and embarrassingly knowing why you have gone back to working in a reactive, short-sighted way. Lucky you.

MIRROR MOMENT

Do you really know what it means to be agile? Does your definition have a tangible, almost sticky sense of measurable conviction? Or is it the kind of gnawing irritation that things just aren't right and you just want to do something–anything–to make things better? Want us to hit another soft spot? If we told you to measure your agility, could you? Or better yet, what would your customers say? Suddenly, all we hear are crickets again....

Don't worry. We'll help you feel better in a minute.

THE HISTORY OF AGILITY SELLING

But if you make the right choices, you will not only be able to harness the chaos, but measure your ability to do so. Through years of both research and experience, we sought to understand why so many sales funnels don't work, why forecasting consistently falls short, why customers don't respond in ways we thought, and why sales organizations don't work together. When we embarked on this quest, we were on two different sides of the country working with different clients in different industries. As so often happens, when we finally connected and started to collaborate, our ideas sparked new thought and debate. We began to see the patterns in our own approach and, through additional testing and research, the new Agility Selling methodology was born.

CONSIDER THIS

There are three major trends creating butterflies in the professional selling world. These trends require Agility Selling. They are increased, or rapidly evolving:

1. Globalization
2. Competition
3. Technology

DEFINING AGILITY SELLING

Simply said, *Agility Selling is a non-linear, pattern-based methodology* for selling. This methodology is designed to help anyone responsible and accountable for revenue generation to cope with the three forces explained in Chapter 1 (the force of the non-linear, the force of full value, and the force of community). The principles of Agility Selling can be applied to any sales situation.

Agility Selling is not a sales technique. Nor is it a sales process. While techniques and processes have value, Agility Selling is bigger than that. It is a genuinely fresh approach to selling, birthed by chaos and grounded in science. Agility Selling is a methodology designed to help you identify repeatable and predictable patterns in the complex world of selling so that you

BUILDING ON THE FOUNDATION

Definitions

The word *sell* is derived from the Icelandic word *selja* and the Anglo-Saxon word *syllan*; both mean "to serve" or "to give." The *American Heritage Dictionary* defines a *sale* as "the exchange of goods or services for an amount of money or its equivalent [or] the act of selling."

A *sale* must therefore be a unique transaction with deliverables and an exchange of money or its equivalent. A transaction is a distinct event in the overall sales process.

A *sales process* is a series of tactical and strategic steps that leads to the sales transaction. Sales processes comprise approaches designed to help the selling organization close more business deals.

A *sales methodology* is an "organizing system" containing the methods and organizing principles underlying a particular art, science, or other area of study.

Note: Agility Selling is a methodology.

can create more value for clients. What exactly do we mean by a methodology? Well, the Oxford dictionary defines a methodology as an "organizing system" containing the methods and organizing principles underlying a particular art, science, or other area of study.

Following the Agility Selling methodology maximizes your ability to identify the best possible alternatives for the customer while recognizing and creating value and driving toward consensus on the best possible alternative within customer agreements. Therefore, a conversation supported by the Agility Selling methodology is very proactive and intentional (not reactive and accidental).

THE RULES OF AGILITY SELLING

The Agility Selling methodology is driven by two simple rules:

1. Instead of focusing on the stages of your sales process, *focus on your selling skills.*
2. Instead of focusing on selling your product or service, *focus on justifying the customer's definition of full value.*

Taken individually, the rules of Agility Selling will definitely give you a lift, even a sustainable increase. Taken as a collective whole, the rules of Agility Selling will completely transform your business. And that is precisely what you need in order to thrive in the chaos.

We'll give you a brief overview of both rules here before we move on to a broader explanation of each in the rest of this book.

Rule 1: Focus on Your Skills

Enter the First Rule of Agility Selling: Instead of focusing on the stages of your sales process, focus on your selling skills.

May we ask a favor? Hold off on your perception of the selling skills required for success for just a moment. Did you know that the definition of selling skills has changed? In other words, if you think selling skills are just concepts like prospecting, negotiating, and handling objections, you are wrong. In fact, we think that the true definition of selling skills has been buried by sales process, and that has actually done more damage than good.

Now do we have your attention?

Think about it. How many of you have been to training that focused on your sales process? How to prospect? Process. How to make a presentation (or use PowerPoint)? Process. Negotiations training? Process. How to fill in the little boxes on your CRM? The process to manage your process. While process is important, does it really help you make sense of the randomness around you? Or is it a crutch to give you a feeling of control? Ouch.

Rule 2: Focus on Justifying Full Value

The Second Rule of Agility Selling: Instead of focusing on selling your product or service, focus on justifying the customer's definition of full value.

Just because you think something is important does not mean that the customer will agree with you. At the same time, the customer may not truly understand the potential value you can provide. You need to know how to justify the value that will benefit both sides of the relationship. That value takes the form of expectations. But if you only focus on expectations, you will get caught up in a series of discussions that have as much of a chance of derailing the value as they do of creating it. You need to know not only how to manage expectations, but how to guide the conversations that are part of every customer relationship in a way that keeps expectations in check and full value at the center of the relationship.

The beauty of Agility Selling is that it is universal and scalable. No matter what your industry, your geography, your size, or even your job title in the company, the rules of Agility Selling apply. Because of its simplicity, Agility Selling is easy to implement. You will actually be able to create greater alignment between people and teams. And because it has been developed for a chaos environment, it will increase your performance by accepting what is not going to go away.

Are you ready for that? Just remember, simple doesn't always mean easy.

Let's get more agile!

Making It Stick

The Top Five Challenges Inventory

Agility Selling offers a new way of approaching your customers. What we have covered in this chapter should provide you a great starting point to begin your journey. Because our goal is to help you sell with more agility, it's important that you take a moment and reflect on the challenges you are facing.

Identify the top five challenges you are facing in sales. To start, you may want to identify challenges in creating and closing new business (for example, prospecting, qualifying and disqualifying opportunities, accelerating sales cycles).

Perhaps your challenges are in your own professional development and skill (competencies, skills, knowledge, and roles).

Or perhaps you are experiencing challenges in understanding exactly what your customers want.

List the top five challenges you are facing today in the space provided below.

•

•

•

•

•

Now that you have identified your top five challenges, put them in rank order, with 1 being the greatest challenge you face, and 5 being the least.

1.

2.

3.

4.

5.

Make a note about this page number. We'll be coming back to this list again in later chapters to see how well you're addressing these challenges.

The Four Habits of Agile Sellers

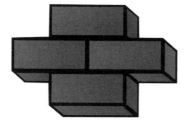

*"Think twice before you speak, because your words and influence
will plant the seed of either success or failure in the mind of another."*

Napoleon Hill

INTRODUCTION

In the last chapter, we explained how seeing patterns where
others see randomness can help you be a more successful
seller. We said that when these patterns are recognized and
the Agility Selling methodology is applied, you will be able to
have more relevant sales conversations with buyers. But because
there is so much change and complexity, it is increasingly difficult
to stay relevant, isn't it?

To handle the change and the complexity, you need to
take stock of what works – and what doesn't. That's a powerful
reason to use the Agility Selling methodology and the patterns
we discuss. Remember, there are two rules to Agility Selling. The

next four chapters we will focus on Rule 1: *Focus on your skills.* Chapters 13 through 17 focus on Rule 2: Instead of focusing on selling your product or service, *focus on justifying the customer's definition of full value.*

Why do we focus on skills first? Because there are fundamental skills that can be applied no matter what the change is or what sales process you use. These fundamental skills allow you to be agile with your customers. Without them, you won't change. In fact, these skills are the ingredients necessary to make any sales process become adaptive and even more focused on the customer. You need these skills in order to drive the right outcomes of your prospecting, negotiating, and follow-up processes. Far too often, we see salespeople focus on their sales process—often at the expense of their customers. In other words, the sales process gets in the way of, and becomes a barrier to, effective communication with the customer. This is why we say to stop focusing on your selling *process* and start focusing on your selling *skills.*

OVERVIEW OF SELLING SKILLS

When we use the term "selling skills," we are talking about what you need to know and what you need to do with your customer, on behalf of your customer, with a focus on driving results and outcomes within your organizational sales culture and, of course, your sales territory. But what if we told you your selling skills can only really support individual activities within the sales process? We discussed the sales process and it's limitations in Chapter 6. How would you respond if we told you your sales process is the wrong design point for building your skills?

That's right, we said it. Your skills are actually more fundamental and more important than to be filtered, and limited, by the sales process. Here's a thought: Isolate the customer and really get to know him or her. To help, picture your top two or three clients in your mind right now. Think of what their needs are. Think about what their challenges are. Think about what drives them. Now think of the skills you need to make each client successful. Think it through. The more you think about it, the more you will realize that, without these skills already in place, the sales process is irrelevant. Without skills, your sales process isn't good enough to help you build true customer intimacy.

Overcoming Obstacles to Skill

> ### CONSIDER THIS
>
> No sales job is without its fair share of problems. If you have been selling for any length of time, you know your attitude toward these problems matters. If you don't have a positive attitude, you're going to have a hard time tackling any problem head on. We know this is easier said than done, but you can do it if you focus on taking one step at a time.

Skills are not easy to build, that's for sure. The sad truth is very few salespeople are trained on professional selling in the way that their peers from other areas of the business are. Marketing colleagues, technology colleagues, and logistics colleagues all have the ability to attain an academic degree in their fields. It's unfortunate that salespeople don't have as many opportunities to earn a degree from a college or university. Luckily, more and more schools are offering professional selling courses and degrees. But what if you aren't fortunate enough to gain an academic degree in selling? You'll have to learn on the job or from your sales training team. That assumes you are learning the right skills. No matter how you look at it, you need to overcome obstacles to developing your skills.

Pause. When it comes to overcoming obstacles to developing skills, you have a choice to make: legs or stairs? By *legs*, we mean your own ability to climb the stairs. Or the hill. Or the mountain. Or whatever obstacle is thrown in your way. By *stairs*, we mean the attempt at turning the obstacle into something more manageable, like carving stairs into the hill or mountain or into whatever obstacle you are experiencing.

This is a big difference between these two choices. Neither will make the obstacle go away. That mountain will still be there. But choosing legs will make the obstacle infinitely easier to deal with. By choosing legs, you can be faster, stronger, more agile. By choosing stairs, you will have clearly defined steps that you can follow, but you will eventually stop climbing and start whining: "This is too hard. It can't be done. My sales funnel is getting clogged. The market is not cooperating. Customers aren't following our steps. They're just not buying. Our price is too high." Oops. Sorry. We switched analogies there.

But you get our point, don't you?

Now, back to our question: legs or stairs? If you choose legs, you're going to need strong legs, and when it comes to strengthening your legs, we've discovered the absolutely best workout. Call it Olympian. Call it world-class. In fact, do call it world-class, because that is what the research set out to define.

For the past few years, we've had the opportunity to work with a fantastic team of people who represented both corporate and academic communities to define world-class selling. It involved more than two thousand people from industries like manufacturing, high-tech, insurance, finance, health care, and government support. We interviewed people from high-performing companies like IBM, Raytheon, Google, and Pitney

BUILDING ON THE FOUNDATION

In 2009, we co-authored the book *World-Class Selling: New Sales Competencies* (Lambert, Ohai, & Kerkhoff, 2009). With this research effort, we led a team to gather input from more than 2,500 professionals who contributed to the creation of 450 competencies, outputs, and behaviors. Collectively, their statements were classified and presented in a model to help individuals build professional selling knowledge and skill. The lasting value of the model is ensured by its broad perspective: It defines the way people operate within the sales system, whether they are directly responsible for revenue generation or support those who are, rather than speaking from a narrow, transaction-based approach. It assumes—and celebrates—the fact that anyone who works within the sales team is a part of its success and, as such, deserves intentional, focused professional development to ensure his or her own success.

Bowes to unknowns of much smaller size. And the study pulled from folks on every continent, except Antarctica, of course. The study is described on the previous page.

THE EMERGING DEFINITION OF SALES PROFESSIONALISM

Through the research we did for the book, we made an amazing discovery. The ability for any salesperson to attain true, professional status actually rests on four fundamental building blocks or skills. These four skills work together to allow freedom, flexibility, adaptability, and quickness at the buyer-seller intersection. They allow agile sellers to stand out and differentiate themselves from all other salespeople in a way that colleagues and customers can appreciate and want to work with. We call these building blocks the "Four Habits of Agile Sellers" because they are not something you can use whenever you feel like it. They are habits you must use *all the time*. They are the bedrock of Agility Selling because, without them, the Agility Selling methodology cannot be effective.

INTRODUCING THE FOUR HABITS OF AGILE SELLERS

The four habits are absolutely the most essential components of what you need to be agile. They are measurable. They are repeatable. They are consistently needed by everyone in the selling organization. From the front line to the back office. From the training room to the executive desktop. And we know that the four habits, when embraced by the organization, can deliver a genuine customer-focused culture that the whole organization can benefit from.

What was most surprising to us when we were conducting the research was that it wasn't the usual list of suspects. Oh sure, we tried. We threw in prospecting, and negotiating, and managing distributors, and the old reliable account management. We tried to shove every aspect of the sales process into the machine to see what came out. And while you will eventually need some of that stuff, none of it is robust enough to touch every aspect of your job and how your customers buy.

The four habits are:

- *Influencing* others through the power of relationships
- Generating *insight* by understanding beyond the obvious
- *Executing* your plan for the full value experience
- Building *credibility* through personal effectiveness

You may be thinking that you knew at least a couple of these already. Great. But did you actually do the math to statistically validate it as part of scientific research? We did, which means that your hunch is something you can literally bet your business on.

MIRROR MOMENT

Here's a mirror moment. When was the last time you went to influence training? When was the last time you strengthened your ability to generate insight by attending an online class? How about excellence through execution training, anyone? Well, at least your personal effectiveness training was completely wrapped within the context of building credibility with your customers, right?

If you don't like your answers to these questions, you are not alone. Literally thousands of salespeople have lamented for years that sales training doesn't actually help them transform their approach to become more relevant with customers.

News flash: If your fundamental selling skills are not in place, sales training is a wasted effort. At best, it can provide a motivational boost to remember what you already knew. At worst, it is a time-sucking activity that pulls you away from your customers.

THE IMPACT OF THE FOUR HABITS

The cool thing about focusing on your skills is that this allows you to get outside the sales funnel, where you can quit being limited to the stages of your sales process. That's right. No matter where you are in creating the full value experience for your customer through *discovering, positioning,* and *delivering* value with your customer, you still need to leverage all of your skills. So no matter what sales process your company uses, these skills can be rolled up into the habits that make you successful. And to that end, the Four Habits of Agile Sellers we discuss in the following chapters will make you better.

In defining the four habits, we worked with thousands of salespeople around the globe. We have found these habits to be a critical ingredient to their success. We also know that it is incredibly helpful to be able to simplify the building blocks of success in an environment that is constantly chaotic. In Brian's book *Ten Steps to Successful Sales* (Lambert, 2009), he wrote:

> *"A lot of what has been missing in professional selling has to do with the lack of a body of knowledge—in effect, the equivalent of* Gray's Anatomy *for the world of selling. In other words, many salespeople don't read books that will help them make the transition to trusted advisor and sales professional. You may notice that selling is more complicated than you thought—or, worse yet, than your organization believes."*

The Four Habits of Agile Sellers are the centerpiece of that body of knowledge Brian talked about. Ignoring them is like ignoring the skeleton in an anatomy class. There's nothing for everything else to hang on. But if these habits are in place, you can literally hang the rest of the selling profession from them.

Whatever process you are trying to use will actually have the foundation to be successful. And when the process is not working as planned, the habits still give you the ability to recognize and transform chaos patterns into actionable steps. For example, if you thought you were negotiating a deal as part of Positioning Your Value when you suddenly found yourself switching into Discovering Value mode, you can quickly tie into your first anchor point (your Sales Fundamentals) with the Four Habits of Agile Sellers.

Here's the kicker. Activities like closing deals and setting sales strategy are worthless if you don't go all-in and radically commit to the four habits of influence, insight, execution, and credibility. Don't tell us you are working to be better at handling objections if you don't have the four habits deeply embedded in your day-to-day activities. Don't tell us that your company is sending the entire sales leadership team through a coaching program if the four habits have not been addressed first. What are you going to coach? Prospecting without influence? Negotiating without insight? Don't waste your time.

Just remember, there are no shortcuts. You need all four of these habits. When it comes to Agility Selling, the four habits are forever interconnected. You cannot take one out and assume that you can still be agile. People think they can be really good with one or two and treat the other habits as "nice to haves." This is not an either-or conversation. That kind of thinking is only going to get you in trouble. Seriously, if we could harness the chaos with one or two habits, we would not have written this book.

Individually, these topics aren't new. We know that. But if we followed you around, looking at the training you went to, the books you read, the websites you visited, would we see that you are focused on the Four Habits of Agile Sellers? Could we tell that your business rests on these habits? Or would we see that you are living a nightmare of defining your day-to-day operations by the stages of a linear sales process?

MIRROR MOMENT

So here's your next mirror moment. Are you a one-trick pony? In other words, do you rely on just one of these habits? If you find yourself pushing a single idea like relationship, consulting skills, follow-through, or any number of personal effectiveness skills (time management, anyone?) over all other skills, you are a one-trick pony.

You may be able to turn on the other habits if you actually choose to, but chances are, your day is determined by your ability to experience the habit you like the most. This behavior is actually contributing to your chaos. If you genuinely want to be agile, you must commit to all four of the habits.

Well, remember the three options you had way back in Chapter 1: work harder, work smarter with the same old tools, or work smarter using a new perspective and new tools? Focusing on your skills is the first step to developing a new perspective. Let's go to the next chapter to learn more.

Making It Stick

Keep, Start, Stop

Perhaps the most important (and most difficult) aspect of selling is understanding your strengths and weaknesses. Not only must you understand what you need to do, but you must also be willing to take action to address any shortcomings. If you're in a good coaching relationship with someone (a sales manager or sales trainer), then you are In a great position to receive developmental feedback. Unfortunately, sometimes you have to take stock yourself. We talked about habits and competencies in this chapter. You need to put these concepts into practice. The key is to critique yourself (and ask others to critique you) in a way that helps you grow.

A simple, yet highly effective, method to use is **the Keep/Stop/Start method**. Ask your coach to help you answer the following questions:

- What do I do that I should keep doing?

- What should I stop doing?

- What am I not doing that I should start doing?

Habit 1: Influencing Others

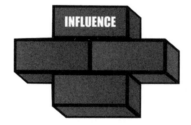

"There is only one way . . . to get anybody to do anything. And that is by making the other person want to do it."

Dale Carnegie

INTRODUCTION

In the last chapter, we explained the Four Habits of Agile Sellers. In this chapter, we go into greater detail with the first habit of *influence*. In the next three chapters, we will explain each of the remaining habits, *insight*, *execution*, and *credibility*, and break them down for you in a similar manner.

What is influence, especially as it pertains to your customer? *Influence gives you the ability to have an effect on people and, ultimately, on results.* Influence is not simply the art of relationships. Relationships give you a cup of coffee. Influence gives you the power to move sales conversations forward.

117

Influence opens closed doors and helps you do stuff through others. It helps you manage individual boundaries, move activities forward, and build alignment. Without influence, you may:

- Struggle in working with others;
- Be boxed into dead-end relationships (especially with customers); or
- Consistently misunderstand how roles are supposed to work together.

If you rely on influence too much, you could be perceived as:

- Manipulative,
- Inappropriately devoted to customers, or
- Constantly trying to control everyone.

As a definition, influence is about the ability to turn social connection into desirable and measurable actions or, in simpler terms, *achieving results through others*. It's the result of conformity (what people do) and motivation (why people do it). Let's unpack this concept of influence and talk about the first ingredient: conformity.

PAY ATTENTION

Influence. It gives you the power of relationship—not simply the art of relationships. Relationships can help you land a huge sale or provide you a cup of coffee from a friend. When it comes to Agility Selling, influence can give you more.

CONFORMITY

The best way to explain conformity is to picture it as three levers. The first lever is Have To, the second lever is Promised To, and the third lever is Want To. Each of these levers is dependent on the buyer's perception of your influence during the course of a sales conversation. When it comes to influencing others, you can use your understanding of these levers to help make the task easier. In other words, conformity provides leverage to get the result.

Taking the buyer's point of view during the conversation, the three levers can be shown as in the graphic.

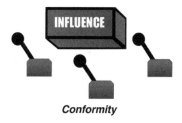

Conformity

The first lever is *have to*. You are pulling the have to lever when the person being influenced is doing what you want him or

BUILDING ON THE FOUNDATION

Dale Carnegie

Dale Carnegie was a U.S. lecturer and author. Born into poverty, he worked as a traveling salesman and an actor before he began teaching public speaking at a YMCA in New York City in 1912. His classes were extremely successful, and he was soon lecturing to packed houses. To standardize his teaching methods he began publishing pamphlets, which he collected into book form as *Public Speaking: A Practical Course for Business Men* (1926). His hugely popular *How to Win Friends and Influence People* (1936) won him a national following; like most of his books, it reveals little that was not known about human psychology but stresses that an individual's attitude is crucial.

Source: Encyclopedia Britannica, Inc. For more information visit Britannica.com.

her to do but doesn't really think that way or "want" to act that way. You will have conformity only as long as you are there. Turn your back, and the other person will stop doing what you want him or her to do. Think of the customer who listens to you only because a supervisor told her to.

The second lever is *promised to.* You are pulling the promised to lever when the person being influenced will do what you want as long as he or she is part of your work group. Someone may even say that he believes in what you want him to do, but this kind of conformity is usually temporary. Once the person leaves the group, he or she will revert to old ways. Think of the customer who is so great to work with until the contract is over. Then he just disappears.

Finally, the third level is *want to.* You have pulled the want to lever when the person being influenced has truly changed his or her mindset and has chosen to align with yours. Whether you are there or not, whether there is a contract or not, the person whole-heartedly agrees with you – and you, as an influencer, have made a lasting impact. Think of the customer who becomes a trusted advisor who helps you protect and even extend your influence.

Obviously, when you exert influence using the "have to" lever, you'll require the most effort during the course of the conversation (many conversations usually). And exerting influence with the "want to" lever is going to be easier during the course of the conversations you have with the buyer. Influencing others to do something they haven't considered before is never that easy, but if you have a lever to take away some of the effort, wouldn't you want to use it to move from conversation to conversation more effectively?

MOTIVATION

The second part of the influence equation is motivation. As stated earlier, motivation is the "why" behind people's actions. If conformity can be seen as levers, motivation can be seen as a set of pulleys that increase your leverage, as shown in the graphic.

Motivation

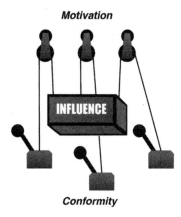

Conformity

The first pulley is *need*. Simply said, people need you (or what you are offering), so their motivation to work with you is grounded in a benefit they will receive from you. Take away the benefit, and the need disappears. You can probably think of a few customer examples of this dynamic on your own.

The second pulley is *like*. It's been said too many times: All things being equal, people do business with the people they like. Being liked goes beyond polite cooperation to genuine, positive regard. If you're in professional sales and don't know this already, you might want to look at a different profession.

The third pulley is *respect*. Respect takes positive regard to a completely different level. When someone respects you, you have established both admiration and trust. People will seek what you have to say and listen to you, even if they don't agree.

PAY ATTENTION

If conformity can be seen as levers, motivation can be seen as a set of pulleys.

PAY ATTENTION

Pause. Trust is a powerful word, and we don't want to just drive past the concept to get to our next habit.

MIRROR MOMENT

Do people trust you? Are you someone customers will listen to, even if they don't agree, because they know you have an ethical core?

Forget your company for a moment (because we know that sometimes your company may be the untrustworthy part of this topic – but that's a separate discussion). Business ethics in sales is a tricky deal. In our experience, no matter the country, the topic of bribes and under the table "requirements" always surfaces. If you are willing to sacrifice trust in the name of the deal, you will never be a true master of influence. And if you cannot master influence, you will never be a true sales professional. 'Nuff said.

CONSIDER THIS

Trust is given to you by your customers and those around you. You can't walk into a room and say "Trust me!" It just doesn't work anymore.

Gaining and earning trust requires authenticity. When it comes to Agility Selling, you must be authentic in your interactions with customers and with your colleagues.

To influence others, you may have to start with yourself. In other words, change your behavior in order to become more aligned with where your customers are going. And then leverage influence to help you get there.

Back to our analogy.

It is amazing how many people think that they only need to work with one pulley. We have seen so many salespeople settle for only one aspect of influence. In short, they are content with need, like, or respect. But, if you remember your high school physical science class, the best use of pulleys is as a complete set, where each pulley works with the others. Then, if you start combining pulleys and levers, you create the power to manage massive obstacles and accomplish unbelievable things. The pyramids of Egypt, anyone?

Increasing influence is about maximizing the conformity and motivation in your relationships. At the very least, you should be

BUILDING ON THE FOUNDATION

Albert Bandura and Motivation

Over a career spanning almost six decades, Bandura has been responsible for groundbreaking contributions to many fields of psychology, including self-efficacy theory, which is the belief that one is capable of performing in a certain manner to attain certain goals. At the heart of influence is the belief that you can make an impact—and that your efforts will make an impact on other people. This theory of motivation is highly studied by academics in professional selling.

A 2002 survey ranked Bandura as the fourth-most-frequently cited psychologist of all time, behind B.F. Skinner, Sigmund Freud, and Jean Piaget, and as the most cited living one. Bandura is widely described as the greatest living psychologist and as one of the most influential psychologists of all time.

When it comes to selling, the belief that we can attain a personal or professional goal leads to motivation. People who are motivated have a desire to undertake their work to the best of their ability. And when it comes to motivation, when we have a desire to achieve a goal, and put forth the energy to work toward that goal, we are said to be "motivated." When it comes to motivating others through influence, you have to give someone a reason or incentive to do something.

able to consciously create relationships where people *have to* work with you because they *need to*. It is not a powerful point of influence, but it is influence nonetheless because you are doing stuff through others. Over time, you may be able to create the kind of ultimate influence where people *want to* work with you because they respect you. Wouldn't that be fun?

For example, have you ever worked with a customer who didn't initially want to work with you? Were you ever able to change the relationship? If you replay the relationship in your mind, you probably used the concepts of conformity and motivation – even if it was accidental.

MANAGING INFLUENCE

Here's a quick thought. Do you consciously try to manage your influence? Do you try to look at your business relationships (both internally and externally) with the kind of critical eye that identifies where your effort to influence is not achieving results? Do you know how to analyze your influence through the lenses of conformity and motivation to break down your business relationships, see the risks, look for patterns, and unlock your personal effectiveness by changing your behavior as necessary? If you are going to harness the chaos, you need to.

Consider Caroline's story. As a key account sales consultant, Caroline had been working with her customer for a couple of years, selling consulting services on a project-by-project basis. It was one of the biggest accounts she had and it was loaded with complexity. Because the account was a large retail chain, the number of relationships she had to manage was an ever-shifting number. On some projects, the customer would have a small team of stakeholders. On other projects, the stakeholders spanned not only departments and functions, but huge chunks of geography. She had been working with one of their specialty departments on their customer relationship strategy when it was announced that the retailer was entering a formal alliance with one of their key suppliers. Unfortunately, the supplier had not only a different philosophy for customer relationship strategy, but also another company on retainer to provide consulting services.

CONSIDER THIS

When it comes to influencing others, here are some things to consider:

- Navigating organizational structures
- Communicating effectively
- Aligning to customers' needs
- Setting expectations
- Negotiating positions
- Building relationships

Source: Brian Lambert, Tim Ohai, and Eric Kerkhoff, *World-Class Selling, New Sales Competencies.* ASTD Press, 2009.

Caroline was being set up for an either/or, win/lose situation. She quickly realized she had better start doing something or she was going to lose her entire project, and possibly the relationship.

Her first job was to understand the level of conformity associated with the alliance. With all corporate announcements, there are public statements of how great everything is going to be and there are private assessments that give a more realistic view on both possibilities and obstacles. In this case, the level of conformity was publicly *want to*, while conversations with her customer network exposed it as much more of a *promised to* (and sometimes even just *have to*) when the executives weren't in the room. This showed Caroline that the alliance had some wiggle room to define how to turn promises into desires.

Her second job was to identify the motivation of the alliance so that, if she was affected by it, she could create leverage and keep her customer. There was high respect between the retailer and the supplier, but opinions about the other consulting company were mixed. On one hand, Caroline's competitor had a high-profile reputation. On the other, the project team was staffed with a bunch of "intelligent" types—MBAs with no real experience. The legitimate consultants had sold the relationship and left it to the junior folks to create reports, PowerPoints, and billable hours. Caroline recorded it as a relationship based on need.

Caroline knew that she had to build a superior position to this promised to/need-based influence and that it was only a matter of time before she would be called to help. What did she do with the time she had? She worked on figuring out suggestions and solutions to convert promised to into want to and intentionally worked on being *liked* and *respected*. Whatever work she did for the customer, she diligently tracked results and made them visible in a way that her customer stakeholders would receive credit for a job well done.

Pause. Did you catch that? Did you see that it wasn't about developing relationships or even about her reputation? It was about developing influence, getting stuff done through others, even if it meant sharing the success in a way that the others received the credit. Caroline knew, and rightly so, that getting all of the credit is short-term thinking. She was thinking long term, and that meant getting all of the *influence*. Once she had that, the short term would be taken care of.

Sure enough, the customer became frustrated with the supplier's consultants and asked Caroline to help sort out the customer relationship strategy for the alliance. Using the same lenses of conformity and motivation, she quickly assessed the supplier's stakeholders and found that everyone but the supplier's chief executive was willing to accept the retailer's approach to customer strategy that she had helped create.

Caroline first had to engage her competitors directly (they were told they had to work with her), which she was able to quickly leverage and take advantage of the position of respect she held through her superior understanding of the problem and her suggestions for converting have to into want to, effectively nudging her competitors to the back seat. Using her newly formed influence with the supplier's staff, she was able to sit down with the supplier's chief executive and discover why he wasn't interested in changing his customer relationship strategy.

Choosing Your Battles

Are you ready for the twist in this story? Caroline was not able to change the chief executive's mind. She had found a place where her influence would not be effective. Many folks would say that was a failure. Was it? Do you always win every battle, even the tough ones that you are pulled into halfway down the road? Is that the true mark of a sales professional?

We would say no. We would say that the market is chaotic and random and that customers use butterflies to create snowstorms. We would also say that a true sales professional would have anchored herself so that she could build influence in a tough situation and create success where none is available. A true sales professional can determine what can be influenced and what cannot. Which is what Caroline did.

Instead of trying to force an either/or, win/lose situation with the supplier's chief executive, Caroline focused on where she had the most leverage. She was able to use her influence to get both sides to agree to disagree. The customer relationship strategy would not change when selling the supplier's products, but the retailer would keep their original customer relationship strategy whenever anything else was sold in that specialty department. Did Caroline win? Absolutely. Not only did she protect her own work from being thrown out the door, but she was able to use the experience as an influence-maker to obtain more business with her original customer and eventually quadruple her total revenue.

In summary, influence is about achieving results through others, using conformity and motivation to do the job. As we said earlier, it is so much more than relationship-building skills. Generating positive regard is nice, but it limits your ability to be agile. If you are going to actually harness the chaos to get something positive out of the situation, you must use influence to do it.

It's really so simple, isn't it? But as we told you in the last chapter: Simple doesn't mean it's easy. And so it is with the next habit.

Making It Stick

Here's an exercise for you. Think of a relationship you need to influence. Perhaps you are fighting with a competitor for a piece of business. Perhaps you are blocked by a controlling purchasing manager who won't let you talk to anyone else. Perhaps it is a case of being lost in the shuffle of personnel at your own organization. Use the two lenses of conformity (what people do) and motivation (why people do it). What do you see? Can you see where you are weak on one or even both areas? Can you see where you need to put your energy to make improvements? Play with ideas in your mind, teasing out ways that you may leverage motivation to gain improved conformity. Go back and forth; talk it out with a co-worker or your manager. Conformity and motivation. Motivation and conformity. Are you starting to see ways to unlock the relationship?

Write them here.

Habit 2: Generating Insight

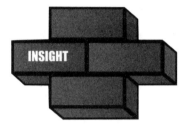

"There is nothing so terrible as activity without insight."

Johann Wolfgang von Goethe

INTRODUCTION

Welcome to the next habit of Agility Sellers: generating insight. Remember, we're still unpacking the first rule of Agility Selling (focus on your skills). But before we jump into explaining how to leverage this second habit, let's digest what we mean by "insight." Insight is a popular word in many sales and marketing organizations. While insight can be used to explain data collected or trends identified, when we think of insight, we mean more than just noticing something. We're also focused on more than becoming aware of or "knowing" something. To us, *insight is the secret of deeply understanding anything—beyond what is obvious.* Insight is seeing beyond the facts in a fresh and innovative way. And guess what? This is what your buyers are looking for from you. This habit of generating insight is really about knowing as much as, if not more than, the person you are talking with. To a certain degree, it is the mystery ingredient or, dare we say secret sauce, of professional selling. Take insight out of your sales conversations, and you are left with a bland, undifferentiated message. Without insight, you are just a talking head. When it comes to talking with your customers without insight, you've got nothing.

If your insight is weak, you may:

- Struggle to consistently identify and categorize critical information,
- Rush to conclusions without gaining real understanding, or
- Be unable to identify risks.

Conversely, if you over-rely on insight, you may:

- Collect too much information,
- Become a victim of "analysis paralysis," or
- Apply your information to the wrong situation.

THE IMPORTANCE OF INSIGHT

Why is insight so vital? It's because, with this habit, you have the jet fuel of decision making. Making decisions without insight leads to a lot of risk, for you and for your customer. As a sales professional, your job is defined by the decisions you make. More importantly, your decisions impact how you work with others. And when it comes to your prospects, they'll only decide to become customers when they decide to work with you. When your prospects become customers, they only stay with you if they decide to stay with you. What's more, your ability to recognize and create value, for better or worse, is directly impacted by the decisions of the people around you. By following the Agility Selling methodology, you can also generate insight on how things are done at your own company. Once you have insight to understand what is truly going on, you can do better than make informed decisions—you can make insightful ones.

INSIGHT OVERRIDING THE SALES PROCESS

Mario was working as a brand new enterprise technology sales-person. Within the first ninety days, he found himself face-to-face with a prospect who represented a substantial new business opportunity. Mario's past sales training, and the coaching advice he had received from the experienced salespeople around him, encouraged him to proceed through the sales process step-by-step in a linear way, starting with "Step 1." He was told to make sure the prospect heard the newly revised presentation on brand value, to ensure the prospect was aware of all the ways the company was unique and different, to prepare a list of canned responses for handling objections, and on and on.... But the worst part? Mario's company told him that they expected this opportunity was going to be a three-call close with a heavy round of negotiations involved some time afterward. You should not be surprised when we tell you that the average sales cycle at Mario's company was four months. But luckily for that company (and the prospect), Mario was more concerned about being agile – and his insight landed him the new deal in less than sixty minutes.

You see, Mario's ability to gather and share insight led to a key decision-point in the sales process. On the very first call, Mario perceived that the buyer was ready, willing, and able to buy a software and data deal worth tens of thousands of dollars. "How can that be?" Mario wondered. After all, he had just met this person, he was ninety days on the job, representing a new solution, and within forty-five minutes, it appeared a major new business deal was well on its way to final agreement. In fact, the prospect had already agreed to the pricing. Mario and the prospect were now talking about implementation and timelines.

How did he do it? Mario asked a simple question. He said; "Mr. Prospect, it appears you know exactly what you want. And forgive me for being blunt, but it seems like we can actually forgo a lot of my presentation. Have you had experience using this software and data package before, or is this something new for you?"

Are you ready for the answer? The prospect had used the exact same combination of software and data at another company. In fact, he had just been hired three weeks before, and he wanted to gain access to the same tools he was so familiar with so that he could make an impact as soon as possible. Wow. Talk about adding some jet fuel to the decision-making process.

BASICS OF GAINING INSIGHT

All right, you say. How do I gain insight?

You just did it. You just asked a question.

Questions are the easiest and most fundamental way to gain insight. Unless you like waiting around for it to drop in your lap because someone else did the asking for you. Don't think you fall into that trap? Here's a test: How many questions did you ask on your last sales call? How many answers did you hear that went beyond a simple "yes" or "no"?

We can't figure out why, if the skill of asking good questions is so vital to business, so many salespeople are so weak (or lazy) at it. Seriously. It is one of the weakest skills we consistently see. Lots of people practice talking, but it's always in the form of a statement. Or they use questions to set up a statement, which then leads to the ageless problem of not listening. And don't get us started on the use of open versus closed questions.

Let's just say that if the bulk of your questions don't begin with the following words, you are probably not as insightful as you think you are. With a nod to Rudyard Kipling, the insight words are:

- What
- Why
- When
- How

- Where
- Who

If you start your questions with any words other than these, you will only hear yes or no answers from customers and prospects. And if you only hear yes or no answers, you probably aren't going past the obvious.

PAY ATTENTION

Start your questions with any words other than What, Why, When, How, Where, or Who, and you will only hear yes or no answers from your customers. If you only hear yes or no answers, you probably aren't going past the obvious.

Pause. Classic, aren't they? These words are so common, even old school. Every sales professional should already have them in their vocabulary. But if you are looking for exponentially better questions, be patient. We have them covered in a later chapter where we discuss having agile conversations with customers.

CHALLENGE YOUR ASSUMPTION

But just telling you to ask better questions so that you can achieve better decisions is really – well – obvious. So if you want to take your insight beyond the obvious, we suggest two guidelines. Like two specialized lenses that sharpen focus and provide clarity, these two guidelines will provide much greater clarity for both the questions and the decisions you are trying to gain insight for. The first guideline is big: Remove assumption. (See figure on the next page.)

"Remove" is an intimidating word, isn't it? Especially if you struggle with insight. We actually debated the right term to use. On one hand we don't want to make it too soft. "Limit" assumption? Weak. "Minimize" assumption? Pathetic. You must have a rigorous, almost hard-core commitment to identifying assumptions. After all, they will destroy and discredit your relationship with the customer. How? Because you will lack critical insight.

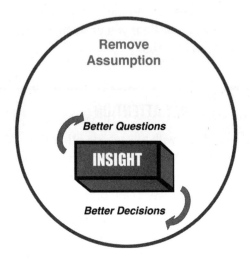

On the other hand, we don't want to be too hard on you. "Eliminate" assumption? Impossible. "Destroy" assumption? That's just silly. Unless you develop the ability to read minds, you will always have to deal with some level of unknown information. And if you are too aggressive, you will actually kill your own intuition, which is never good. Sometimes it is those intuitive hunches that kick the customer relationship wide open.

To create the right interpretation of assumption here, let's say that assumption is never just a single piece of information. In fact, we think assumption is actually a *collection of information bits that occurred at specific moments in time*. While the interpretation of each information bit made sense at the time, that collective interpretation probably doesn't hold true today. Worse, assumptions may have been built on the wrong interpretation of that collective information. In other words, the original analysis of the information was flawed—leading to a poor assumption. So when we say "remove" assumption, we are talking about identifying where the assumptions are and plucking them out so a more accurate view of reality can develop. To explain this process, let's go to Japan.

The Book of Five Rings is a classic explanation of the samurai's approach to battle. Think of it as the Japanese version of the more popular *Art of War*. Written by Musashi Miyamoto, it details five spheres, or rings, that a warrior should master when engaging the enemy. We love it because it is full of metaphors that apply to professional selling. One of the best lessons is called the "Sphere of Emptiness." It describes how one must empty his or her mind and intentionally separate what does and does not exist from what is known and not known to accurately see reality. Did you catch what that means? It means that you have to know which data is actually confirmed and which data is just assumed. There is a difference between what you think you know and what you have actually proven. This process of separation is vital to the person who wants to master insight. If you cannot separate information in this manner, you will never be able to *remove* your own assumptions.

BUILDING ON THE FOUNDATION

The terms "strategy" and "tactics" are widely used in books and articles about management. Sometimes they seem to mean the same thing, and sometimes they seem to have completely different meanings.

Although "strategy" and "tactics" are defined in many different ways, there are some points on which all of the definitions agree: both terms were first used in the military and both are concerned with deciding the means used to achieve a specific goal. For a soldier, *strategy* is about deciding under which terms and conditions an army will fight a battle, whereas *tactics* are about how best to organize an army during that battle. The military historian B. H. Liddell Hart defines strategy as "the art of distributing and applying military means to fulfill the ends of policy."

As Fred Nickols observes, delete the word "military" from this definition and you have your first insight into how the concept of strategy is used in the business world.

Put it this way: In the absence of information, people typically create their own. For example, if you don't know why a competitor is doing something, just create your own reasons for it. If you don't know why a customer refuses to budge on a negotiation, just create your own reasons for it. If you don't know when a deal will close, just guess. Then put it in your forecast—because you don't want to sound as though you don't know your own business, right?

You see, it's human nature to take the bits of information we have in front of us and skip over the parts where we have gaps. We basically assume that if we don't know something, it doesn't exist.

PAY ATTENTION

When it comes to generating insight, here are some things to consider.
    How well do you:

- Analyze organizational forces?
- Understand the customer's business?
- Evaluate customer experiences?
- Gather intelligence from multiple sources?
- Prioritize stakeholder needs?
- Identify alternative options?
- Build a business case?

Source: Brian Lambert, Tim Ohai, and Eric Kerkhoff, *World-Class Selling: New Sales Competencies.* ASTD Press, 2009.

Think about it. How often do people assume that because they don't know something, it must not exist at all? Talk about flawed thinking. Early explorers assumed the world was flat. So for centuries they never ventured far enough to discover new lands. Bringing this concept home to the sales world, a salesperson may try to sell something to a new customer because that customer looks and acts just like a previous customer. The salesperson assumes the customer doesn't want something new or different (or dare we say, more expensive). Think about the ramifications of these assumptions on the sales conversation. Or perhaps a salesperson may think everything is great with a big customer because he is not hearing any complaints. No news is good news, right? Wrong. A true sales professional would never assume that silence is a good thing. He would discover for himself whether the things he doesn't know either exist or do not exist. He would never just create his own information.

MIRROR MOMENT

Mirror moment. Are you a sales professional when it comes to the habit of insight? How well do you manage your knowledge of what is known/not known and what exists/does not exist? Do you do it on purpose, or does it just happen? And, better yet, do you write these things down?

Please don't tell us that you just keep it all in your head, crammed together with all the insights you have collected previously. For every customer. All at one time. Ouch. But we digress.

EXPANDING YOUR PERSPECTIVE

Let's move on to the second guideline: expanding your perspective.

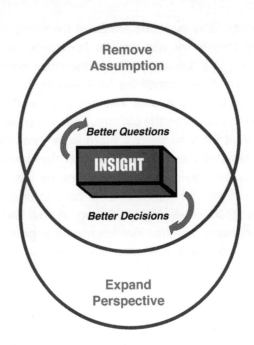

Some people call it "getting above the situation." Others call it "going outside the box." When you expand your perspective, you pull away from the information as if you were no longer a participant in the story. You gather an accurate picture of what is true—without projecting your personal bias. To formulate this new truth, you need to consciously take stock of what you know about the situation with a critical and objective eye. The problem is that you may still overlook something you have missed a hundred times before because assumption is still at work.

So how do you fix this?

We suggest you also expand your perspective by gathering other people's opinions on what they believe to be true about the situation. We know, we know, you're going to have to get over your fear of losing control of the deal by bringing someone else in. (Control is a myth, remember?) Just look at it this way. You're getting some help to land the big fish. Bring your manager in. What does he or she think is true? Grab a teammate from the back office and invite him or her on a sales call to provide an assessment of what you believe to be true. Another way to expand your perspective is to leverage a trusted relationship at your customer's location to bounce your insights off of him or her. Generally speaking, you will want to hear at least two other people's perspectives by asking what they believe to be true. We have found that if you can bring at least three people's perspectives (including your own) to a problem, you can collectively identify patterns and exceptions. *Patterns* will be the things that at least two of you see consistently. *Exceptions* will be the things that one person saw just one time.

As you work to identify patterns and exceptions, make sure that everyone is working to remove his or her personal assumptions and keeping you all focused on the problem. If you hear someone starting to create her own information by projecting personal bias, point it out. Separate what does and does not exist from what is known and not known. Empty your mind of assumptions and fill it with insight.

Collect insight from as many places as possible. Otherwise, you will end up like Craig and Megan.

MULTIPLE SOURCES: GAINING INSIGHT

Craig had been selling automotive supplies to his customer for years. In fact, he had done such a great job with this particular customer that he had developed a genuine friendship with their purchasing manager. Craig consistently scheduled appointments around lunch so that he could meet with the purchasing manager and catch up on personal news while discussing business. They went to sporting events together. Craig even made sure that whenever his company was doing a promotion and giving away free stuff, his colleague received the materials first.

The insights Craig received from his friend were invaluable. He always knew what was going to happen before it happened. Until his colleague was laid off. Suddenly, Craig's insights dried up. Within a year, his relationship with that account grew cold, because Craig didn't have another relationship built up. The good thing was that Craig worked hard to be present within the account. He still joked with people and visited the customer's leadership. But he didn't develop any new insights. He had always relied on his friend to give insight away, and Craig didn't know who to approach to restore the flow of information.

Can you see the risks?

Now look at Megan's story.

Megan was a new sales rep for a software company, and she was trying to manage her first big account. Megan was quickly able to sit down with her account's top leader and have open and frank discussions. The new product she had been tasked with selling was going to require some changes from her customer, but she was pretty convinced that the top leader was on board with making the changes. He was always open and positive when they spoke about what the new product could do for his business. Imagine her surprise when that same leader told her that he was going to pass on making the purchase. Apparently, he was going to buy a similar product from her competitor because it did not require any changes.

Can you see where Megan is making the same mistake that Craig made?

CONSIDER THIS

An assumption is anything that can be taken for granted. If there's one thing we're trying to tell you about selling, it's that you can take very little for granted. Never assume you know enough about your customers. Never assume you know what is going to happen next. Never assume you have all the information you need. Instead, do your best to prove it.

In both stories, the salesperson made the mistake of limiting the flow of insight to just one source. Craig was getting great insight from his single source, but he had no backup plan. Megan, besides doing a poor job of collecting insight, had mistakenly assumed that the information she was collecting from her single source was complete.

If you want to grow, and even protect, your business, do not limit yourself to a single source of insight. Rather, put your energy into looking for insight in as many places as you can. Anyone who has attended a key account selling course will tell you that you must connect with folks at a variety of levels. If you are selling to a large, complex customer, make sure that you have plugged into the high-level executives, the mid-level managers, and the front-line players. What the front line will tell you will likely be different from what the executives will tell you. But if you can obtain information from both sources, combined with the mid-level managers' input, you can create a big picture view of the full value the customer is likely needing. It works the same way with smaller customers who may only have a couple of decision-makers. The full value is always bigger than what one source can tell you. They are still part of a community, so look at how the community interacts to make a decision.

INSIGHT AND SNOWFLAKES

Perhaps the easiest way to explain insight is to use your knowledge of snowflakes.

Remember how customers form snowflakes by the unique combination of their driving needs through the full value experience? Ask yourself: Who drives the *discovery* of value, who drives the *positioning* of value, and who drives the *delivery* of value? And what data are they using to form their own perceptions? What assumptions are *they* making? Did they see or hear something that you haven't seen or heard? Collect insight. By focusing on each stage of snowflake development, you can begin to identify potential sources of insight that you can analyze. You may even uncover things that your customer had no idea were there.

Think of a customer you are struggling with right now. Where is your greatest amount of insight coming from? Which part of the snowflake is giving you the most valuable information? Which part has the least clarity? Chances are, if you have blind spots, you are likely limited to only one source of insight (if that) in that part of the snowflake.

> # MIRROR MOMENT
>
> How often do you only look for insight during one stage of the full value experience? Or worse, do you limit the insight you collect from that one stage in order to sell only your product or service, not the full value your customer is actually looking for. Seriously, how often do you narrow your data collection to just the things that help position you to sell something? Have you ever stopped yourself before positioning one piece of value to ask questions that might help you increase the value you can offer to a customer in another stage?

Remember all the things a customer can complain about? At the very minimum, you should be removing assumption and expanding perspective for each of these topics as well.

It goes right back to snowflakes. If you truly understand how snowflakes form, you will constantly be looking for insight.

INSIGHT AND FORCES OF COMPLEXITY

And if you can remember to keep an eye open for patterns that might randomly appear, you will find yourself looking for insight at any time, about any topic, and from any person. You can apply your insight to any of the chaos patterns, not just the "discovery"phase of your sales funnel. We've been talking about insight

> # CONSIDER THIS
>
> When it comes to insight, you need to spend more time researching your customers. The more knowledge of your customers you have, the more insight you will have. Study the market trends that impact your customers. Understand the external forces that influence your customer's decision making.

and snowflakes, but insight will also tell you when a butterfly is about to appear because you already understand the conditions that create them. And insight will tell you when to reset one of your anchors because you understand the signs that your anchor point is starting to shift. Insight is a pretty valuable habit, isn't it?

Here's our summary. Remove assumption by forcing yourself to separate what you "know" from what you can prove. *Don't assume anything.* Expand your perspective, even if it means you have to bring someone else into "your" deal. Then use your knowledge of snowflakes (and other patterns) to look for insight from as many places as possible. Any time, any topic, and any person.

Ready for your next habit? C'mon. Let's figure out how we can start taking action and executing on your plan.

Making It Stick

Think about your most important customer. When is your next meeting to either talk with or about them? Remember, you may be talking with your own internal team about how to support this customer.

Using your knowledge of how the full value experience (the snowflake) exposes different driving needs at different points of time, what aspect of full value should you be emphasizing now?

Now answer the following questions:

- Is your answer beyond the obvious? Do you know as much if not more than the customer here?

- How do you know? Have you proven it?

- Who else may have insights about this customer need? How could you prove that person's answers?

- Based on your insights, what are your next steps?

You can apply the same general process to other chaos patterns, like looking for butterflies (in each area of PTER) and the strength of your anchor points.

CHAPTER

Habit 3: Executing Your Plan

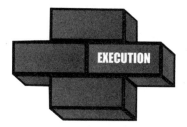

"Good management is the art of making problems so interesting and their solutions so constructive that everyone wants to get to work and deal with them."

Paul Hawkin

INTRODUCTION

The third of the Four Habits of Agile Sellers is *execution*. Before we can go any further, we need to define this concept.

According to Webster's dictionary, the kind of execution we are talking about is basically "the act . . . or result of performance." Ok, that's a start, but we want to go further. Depending on whom you talk to, execution will be bundled along with the concepts of hard work, discipline, accomplishment, and even a bit of luck. We do not disagree with those ideas. On the contrary, we love them.

EXECUTION DEFINED

To us, execution means creating and implementing your plan for the full value experience (remember the snowflakes?). You have to organize the customer's experience. This requires you to develop a strategy to effectively engage the buyer and generate support for the solutions you are communicating. In other words, execution covers how you *discover, position,* and *deliver your value.* Most importantly, the concept (as we define it) explicitly describes how you plan to coordinate mutually agreed-on expectations of what you promised your customer, with the outcome being measurable business results—that you receive credit for.

PAY ATTENTION

We often find the most precious commodity for any salesperson is his or her time. Personal time, and how it is used, can make or break a sales career. While many interpret time management as a critical component of execution, top-performing salespeople take time out to think things through and plan. The mental discipline to take complex challenges and break those challenges down into parts that can be managed is a critical element of execution. You can add value to your team, and to your customer, by showing how much you think things through before acting.

If you are weak in execution, you may:

- Not be able to position solutions effectively,
- Not handle people and resources competently, or
- Be unable to measure outcomes.

Put too much energy into execution, and you may:

- Try to micromanage every aspect of a solution,
- Hoard responsibility, or
- Smother the decision-making process.

WHY EXECUTION IS IMPORTANT

As you may recall from Chapter 4, "full value" is defined as the entire bundle of needs that drive the buyer. We prefer to use the term "expectations" instead of needs because you may see a need that the buyer has no expectation to address. And you can miss other customer expectations as a result of looking for uncovered needs.

Therefore, from this point on, whenever you read the term "full value," define it is your mind as *the entire bundle of expectations that drive the buyer through discovering, positioning, and delivering value.* It is not your products or service. In fact, we are going to stop mentioning products or services. From now on, you sell full value because buyers want far more than your products and services. They want their expectations met for everything associated with the full value experience.

Why do you have to know this? Because by using the habit of execution you are constantly uncovering expectations. Lots of them. We'll talk in greater detail about these expectations later, but for now, let's focus on what you do with them.

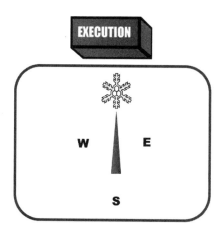

The habit of execution is very much like using your own portable street navigator with a built-in global positioning system (GPS). If you've ever used a street navigator in your car, you know how precious they can be in saving you valuable time. But their most amazing value is helping you get back on the right path after you are detoured or become lost.

BUILDING ON THE FOUNDATION

Project Management

The *Project Management Book of Knowledge* (PMBOK), compiled by the Project Management Institute (PMI), defines project management as "the application of knowledge, skills, tools, and techniques to project activities to meet project requirements."

There are nine knowledge areas for effective project management:

1. Project Integration Management
2. Project Scope Management
3. Project Time Management
4. Project Cost Management
5. Project Quality Management
6. Project Human Resource Management
7. Project Communications Management
8. Project Risk Management
9. Project Procurement Management

Source: Project Management Book of Knowledge (3rd ed.). Project Management Institute, 2004.

Let's transfer the street navigator/GPS analogy to sales. You must have a destination in mind when you are working with customers. This destination is the full value experience you want to deliver to the customer. In your quest to successfully arrive at your destination, you also have to know your current location. The knowledge of both is defined by the full value experience. Yes, your customer wants every expectation addressed. And yes, expectations will be uncovered as you discover, position, and deliver value, so you must develop a plan to address all of it—including detours.

But knowing how to read whether you are lost or not and actually doing something about it are two completely different things. You need both concepts to work together. The habit of execution requires you to constantly check the customer's snowflake to determine whether you are on course, then work with your strategies and plans (for example, territory plans, account plans, etc.) to either remain on course or make any needed corrections. In effect, you must use your knowledge of the patterns you see within the chaos to figure out what is going on, determine next steps, and keep momentum moving toward your desired impact.

CONSIDER THIS

When salespeople sell, they should always ask two important questions about their own personal ability to execute. They are:

1. Where am I with this buyer's snowflake (discovering, positioning, or delivering value)?
2. What do I need to do next with this buyer?

The answers to these questions provide momentum for daily activities. By understanding both where you currently are and where you need to be, you operate tactically. Tactical behavior is good in professional selling . . . just don't forget to take the time to think things through.

Frankly, we could almost use the concept of project management as a partial definition of execution. Project management is about the coordination of plans, resources, and information to get something done. In this case, the "something done" is the full value experience. And if you think you can manage the full value experience (and your territory and account plans) without project management skills, you are clearly not operating with an understanding of what your customers want in today's economy.

WHY YOUR CUSTOMERS EXPECT EXECUTION

When your customers talk about the skills they associate with execution, they bring up things like building a strategy for delivering what you promised, creating feedback loops that allow them to both provide and receive up-to-date information on how things are going, and defining clearly outlined rules for how timelines and budgets will be respected. In fact, your customers expect these skills. And they are not limited to external applications; internal applications are just as vital. Your own selling community may want to know your strategy, feedback loops, and rules for timelines and budget. They may even have some expectations they want to give you. An agile sales professional knows all of this and builds others' expectations into her plans for creating and implementing the full value experience.

MIRROR MOMENT

Mirror moment. Do you build these expectations into your customer plans?

Let's be honest here. Most of us do not like paperwork. And most of us do not like being put into a box. We are not talking about putting you in a box. We are talking about putting your whole self into executing what you promised to your customers. And this means that you will have to plan for the unexpected. What kinds of things create the unexpected? You can probably guess our answer.

Patterns—more specifically, pattern-generated detours. Butterflies get in the way, anchor points suddenly become loose, and snowflakes start to disintegrate. Isn't it amazing how these patterns keep popping up? But since you know these patterns exist (and will keep on existing), how are you planning for when they suddenly appear and take on a life of their own? Do you even force yourself to look for them on a regular basis. And if you find a pattern-generated detour, what are your steps for addressing it?

THREE STEPS TO EXECUTION

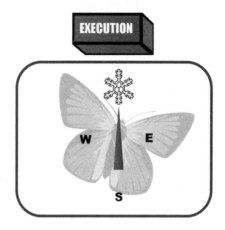

Look at the graphic above. Do you see how the butterfly has been added to the background? This butterfly represents all pattern-generated detours. Pattern-generated detours should be part of your GPS programming. You need to expect these detours in the chaos. We suggest you build your territory and account plans to include at least three steps for dealing with detours: *confirm, analyze,* and *prioritize.*

First, confirm it is actually a pattern-generated detour. Don't assume anything. Even as we write this, Tim had a very big customer go silent for almost a month. The issue was actually a technological one. The customer's email and voicemail accounts were corrupted and they weren't receiving Tim's messages. No butterfly was there, the anchor points settled back down, and the snowflake was stable. No detour occurred, so he went right back to working his plan.

Second, spend some time to analyze the detour until you pinpoint its cause. Use your knowledge of the patterns. As we discussed in earlier chapters, the chaos patterns have some sort of underlying logic at work. Butterflies are created when there is a disruption to people, time, energy, and resources. Anchor points disappear when they are not secured in the right order. And snowflakes begin to disintegrate when the entire bundle of expectations that drives the buyer is being missed or ignored. The root cause of your detour is most likely going to be one of these issues.

Case in point: On another deal Tim was working on, the main customer contact was having trouble obtaining the final signature on a contract because the signer was out of the country on business. It turns out that the trouble had nothing to do with the contract signer being out of the country. Suddenly a butterfly appeared. In this case, the signer was the ultimate decision-maker and had not been properly briefed on the deal. Tim had to readjust (and basically start over). Fortunately, Tim had planned for this possibility in advance and continued working as if it were an intended part of the process.

Third, prioritize the detours you can address. Remember, you can't control the chaos. But you also cannot harness all of the patterns at one time. If you try to do that, your execution will likely suffer. Therefore, ask yourself which detours will create the biggest impact and work with them first. The other problems will have to wait. At the very least, this will help you protect the wins you executed from the losses you experienced.

PAY ATTENTION

Careful preparation and planning are the key to any successful sales conversation. If you don't invest the time to prepare and plan, you will not sell with agility.

When it comes to executing your plans, here are some things to consider. How well do you:

- Facilitate change?
- Formalize agreements?
- Resolve issues?
- Manage projects?
- Leverage success?
- Articulate value?

Three steps: confirm, analyze, and prioritize. Build these steps into your plans. Allow yourself the freedom to adjust your plans based on the best impact of your full value.

BUILDING ON THE FOUNDATION

Execution

The book *Execution: The Discipline of Getting Things Done* inspires action. The authors, Larry Bossidy and Ram Charan, define execution as "a systematic process of rigorously discussing how's and what's, questioning, tenaciously following through, and ensuring accountability." By focusing on execution and framing it as a discipline, the authors show how to tackle the source of many organizational problems that often go unnoticed and unattended.

To execute, the authors define seven essential leadership behaviors:

1. Know your people and your business.
2. Insist on realism.
3. Set clear goals and priorities.
4. Follow through.
5. Reward the doers.
6. Expand people's capabilities.
7. Know yourself.

Source: Larry Bossidy and Ram Charan, *The Discipline of Getting Things Done.* New York: Crown Business, 2002.

RESPONDING TO CHAOS WITH EXECUTION

But here's the catch. Just as you won't always have influence and insight, reality says that you won't always be able to execute your full value. By the very dynamics of Sales Chaos, you will have moments when your perception of the value your customer is expecting will look shaky—or even disappear on you.

Are we making you cringe? We hope not, but if we are, we have some suggestions. Become a butterfly. Start looking for ways to create momentum with your own team. Look for the patterns that you can still address. Leverage your influence to share (and even acquire) insight to the point at which you can get your execution back on track. Remember, the force of community is constantly in motion. If you don't have time for connecting with your internal selling community to harness the chaos, you may need to rethink how you are spending your time. At the very least, make sure you are managing the full value for your top current customers and top targeted customers. Find the customers who will benefit most from your offering and start managing value in small amounts. Grow those small wins as large as you possibly can.

Some of you reading this just had an a-ha moment. One of the chief ingredients to execution is determining who takes your time. Interesting idea, isn't it?

Pause. Is execution an area of development for you? Not sure? Try this.

Analyze your customer portfolio. Identify which customers make up 80 percent of your overall business going forward. You will probably have a fairly short list. If you handle only one customer, follow this same approach based on product line, location, strategic revenue, or whatever makes the most sense to you. Having a short list is vital because it will help you separate your business from your business. Remember, time spent on a customer does not define a top customer. Strategy and revenue do.

Take your list and look at how well each customer is working with you to discover value, position value, and deliver value. Are you involved in all three components of the full value experience? You should be able to see what value your customer wants and how you provide it. You should also be able to see where you have strengths, weaknesses, and opportunities.

If your skill is high, you will have already made a habit of uncovering expectations and setting up plans to manage them. In this case, you can say that you consistently monitor the full value experience so that you can measure progress and results, even sharing them with your customers so that their expectations are not just understood, but fulfilled. These are the hallmarks of a strong execution habit.

If you have no clue what to do or where to start after your analysis, you have just discovered your need. Work on your execution skills. Start becoming a student of the snowflake so that you can determine where you should be going, where you are, and what you need to do to get where you want to be.

Unfortunately, and far too often, we see a salesperson blame his or her organization because the expectations of discovering/positioning/delivering value were never properly managed by that salesperson to begin with. If this is you, don't be so critical of your own organization until you have put yourself under the same microscope. If you assume that things will be done simply because you *expect* them to be done, you are not executing your full value. Frankly, you are not even offering value with this approach. You're just offering hope. And you have turned what could possibly be a decent full value offering and gutted it until it has became a spaghetti noodle. Do you know what we mean? We mean a sales pitch that gets thrown against the wall of a customer's office to see whether it will stick. If that's you, stop. Stop now. And don't do it again.

Before we close out the chapter, let's pause for a quick temperature check. How are you doing? We've hit three of the four habits pretty hard. Are you feeling any pinches? Perhaps your head and heart are arguing over the reality of your day-to-day existence and the ambitions of the world you want to sell in? We hope so. We hope you are having a downright brawl in your mind over what you are (or are not) doing and what you should be doing. At the end of the day, it is going to be a matter of choice. You will either choose to use the Four Habits of Agility Sellers to secure your anchors or choose to compromise your professionalism so you can continue to collect a paycheck from whatever the chaos spews at you. Honestly, the choice is completely yours. Just remember: your choice, your consequence.

Ok. Break's over. Let's get to our last habit.

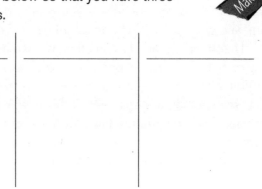

Making It Stick

Think of the last three customers you have interacted with. Write them below so that you have three different columns.

_____ | _____ | _____

Now write your answers to these two questions under each column.

1. Where am I with this buyer's snowflake (discovering, positioning, or delivering value)?

2. What do I need to do next with this buyer?

Next, look for any potential pattern-generated detours in each situation.

1. Are any of your anchors starting to come loose?

2. Are any butterflies starting to appear?

3. Is it possible that the next part of the snowflake that you will spend time on will not be "the next logical" step?

Based on your answers to these questions, do you need to change any of your original answers to the question: What do I need to do next with this buyer? Do it now.

Habit 4: Building Credibility

"If things seem under control, you are just not going fast enough."

Mario Andretti

INTRODUCTION

The fourth habit is a bit strange. Well, maybe the word "different" is a better choice, because it actually enlarges the impact of the other three habits we already discussed. You can have influence, insight, and execution, but if you are lacking in the credibility category, you are probably not experiencing the kind of success you expect from your daily activities and interactions with your customers.

PERSONAL EFFECTIVENESS = CREDIBILITY

The demonstration of credibility requires personal effectiveness. Why? Because credibility is the result of *taking responsibility for all the relationships, processes, and methodologies within your day-to-day selling activities.* If you are not able to consistently prove yourself as dependable and reliable, your reputation will slowly diminish. On the other hand, we've seen many salespeople break down barriers just by "being professional." In order to harness the chaos of today's selling reality, credibility is mandatory.

If credibility is a true habit for you, you are good at communicating, protecting your ethics, embracing diversity, and managing your time. You know how to link your technology, learning, and non-selling activities to your business. You effectively solve problems and use processes to make your success repeatable. In short, you not only do stuff, but you do it well.

Pause. We want to highlight, italicize, and underline the context of professional selling. At this point in time, we don't want you think about your home life. Don't think about your office life. Focus on the life you live that is wrapped up in how customers buy and what you have to do to get those buying decisions to happen – again, and again, and again. Wrapped up? Try covered, smothered, and dripping with it.

The signs that you are weak in this area include:

- Consistently missing deadlines,
- Taking too long to get "on track," or
- Not grasping how your personal activity links to revenue.

You may be overly reliant on credibility if you:

- Spend too much time on projects,
- Dismiss (or alienate) other people for not being as efficient as you are, or
- Ignore other critical business priorities if they do not directly produce revenue.

See how this one habit pushes into the other habits? To be fair, you can be a person of modest influence without having a high degree of credibility, but you are severely limiting your influence (and your insight and execution). At the same time, it is almost impossible to build credibility without it affecting and improving your other habits.

Look at the graphic above. Notice how credibility is releasing that big plus sign? When credibility is working the way it is supposed to, it adds substance to your other efforts. The plus sign represents that added substance. This is what we mean when we say that credibility enlarges the impact of your other habits.

Think about it. What will credibility do for your execution activities? Your insight activities? Surely you see how influence is impacted by credibility. In fact, we will go so far as to say that you will never achieve true mastery of the other habits until you have achieved mastery in your credibility.

To be fair, the things that define credibility are not new. What worked a hundred years ago (mostly) work today. Communicate well, solve problems, be ethical, and learn fast. Now add in the more modern concepts like time management and embracing diversity. You are most of the way there. But we are not simply trying to remind you of these things. We want you to become a master of them. Just like Stephen learned to be.

CONSIDER THIS

These days, first impressions often don't happen face-to-face. They can occur online in Google searches conducted weeks before a potential meeting. Because it is virtually impossible to keep your personal life and professional image separate online, you need to think about managing your "online reputation" using search engines, websites, portals, and blogs. While the face-to-face meetings and interactions with peers and customers are still important, you must be aware of how you're perceived personally and virtually.

The Importance of Credibility

Stephan was assigned to the bustling market of Los Angeles. He was a fairly new sales representative, but that did not mean that he didn't know what he was doing. Quite the contrary. With the successes he was quickly notching under his belt, he was developing quite a reputation as a sales pro of the future.

He was also developing a reputation as a pain. His manager was a veteran of the company, and he didn't like the "new kid." From Stephan's perspective, this manager was worse than a dinosaur. He was an over-inflated, completely isolated, incompetent waste of managerial salary. To say that the manager lacked in credibility was an understatement. Consequently, Stephan had shut off his manager, thinking he would just go about his business and sell like crazy.

The problem was that Stephan was losing all of his own credibility at the home office. The word that his manager was spreading through the LA office rumor mill was that Stephan was the egomaniac and that Stephan's days were numbered. Stephan was about to become a victim of his own effectiveness – or rather his overly developed effectiveness.

Can you see where Stephan was going wrong?

He was overextending his strength. He was intelligent, hardworking, and ethical. He had strong communication skills and even knew how to use laughter as a precious resource. Stephan's credibility was a point of pride for him. Yet he did not know how to dial it back to just controlling his own body.

CONSIDER THIS

Balance means a point between two opposite forces that is desirable over one state or the other, such as a balance between the metaphysical law and chaos – law by itself being overly controlling, chaos being overly unmanageable, balance being the point that minimizes the negatives of both.

Source: Retrieved October 1, 2010, from http://en .wikipedia.org/wiki/Balance.

If you will allow us a short detour, we'd like to show you something that will help you understand this concept of credibility even better.

BALANCE

You have probably noticed that the Four Habits of Agile Sellers are listed with both "weak" and "overly reliant" indicators. We did this because weaknesses are often strengths that have been over-extended. Take any of these habits, and you will quickly see how they must be calibrated and centered on the scale of use so that they remain useful.

We call this *balance*. When it comes to the Four Habits of Agile Sellers, balance is much more than a guiding principle. Balance is a natural state within selling because it a natural law of business, a law you must obey without question, hesitation, or doubt. If you don't, you will not only lose the agility you are trying desperately to achieve, but you will hit the ground hard—and take others with you.

In Agility Selling, balance can be demonstrated in one of two ways. The first defines the requirements of how you use your four habits. The second has to do with making sure all four habits are in play.

The First Demonstration of Balance

The first demonstration of balance is to *make sure that the four habits are used with a healthy sense of boundaries*, as in I influence you, but not too much. I share my insight with you, but not too much. And so on. The principle works exactly like a carpenter's level. Move too far to the right or left, and the bubble in the glass vial shoots askew. You have to keep the bubble within the boundaries marked on the tool.

This first demonstration of balance is so important because boundaries are a central part of healthy working relationships. Being able to work *with* someone is far more effective than having someone work for you, because if you cannot work with people, those same people will stop working with you. Golden Rule, anyone?

BUILDING ON THE FOUNDATION

The Golden Rule: Treat others as you want to be treated.

The Golden Rule is endorsed by pretty much all of the great world religions; Jesus, Confucius, and Hillel used it to summarize their ethical teachings. And for many centuries the idea has been influential among people of very diverse cultures. These facts alone suggest that the Golden Rule may be an important moral truth.

Source: H.J. Gensler, *My Formal Ethics.* London: Routledge, 1996.

Back to Stephan. Fortunately for him, one of the other sales managers (Jim) saw what was going on and stepped in. Jim saw the potential Stephan had, and he saw how Stephan was killing his own career. He pulled Stephan aside and told him that there would always be ineffective people to deal with—he just couldn't let them become a distraction. Jim arranged for Stephan to transfer from Los Angeles to a grittier territory in Orange County so he could get a fresh start and renew his focus. A year and a half later, Stephan was no longer the egomaniac. Instead, he was up for a promotion.

But not everyone is so lucky as to have someone come along to explain the first demonstration of balance.

We also knew a guy named George. George was an experienced salesperson, working a territory that he had come to virtually own. Over time, and through a lot of hard work, he had grabbed every significant piece of business that existed. There were no new opportunities that he didn't already have a finger in. Unfortunately, the success went to his head. Somehow, he thought that the success was all because of him, not the community he belonged to. He stopped listening to folks at the home office, ignored the requests by his manager to work with marketing on special projects, and got into a bad habit of always asking his co-workers for favors without offering to do any for them. Without knowing it, he lost whatever influence/insight/ execution/credibility he had once worked so hard to obtain. The bubbles on his leveling tool were all horribly skewed.

Time passed and the market changed. In addition to the people George knew moving on to other roles, customer needs evolved and required him to renew his value. The problem was that George couldn't deliver what he promised because his customer community grew faster than he could keep up with. His lack of balance took over. Responsibilities were being missed and butterflies started appearing out of nowhere. George's once ironclad grip on his territory slowly crumbled as his competitors started acquiring his best customers. And because he had become disconnected to his own selling community, he no longer knew whom to call when he needed help. And what did he get when he called the home office generic help line for last-second support for a top customer on a Friday afternoon? Voicemail.

And people wonder why the profession of sales gets such a bad reputation internally.

The Second Demonstration of Balance

Now, don't forget, there is a second demonstration of balance. The second is to *make certain that all four habits are in play.* If you remember, our research showed that every one of the four habits is vital to your ability to carry out the rest of your job. Need to manage your sales strategy? The four habits apply. Need to protect your accounts? Not without the four habits, you don't. Need to coach for sales results, deliver sales training, or even support indirect selling? The four habits are all essential.

If you find yourself focusing on one habit too much, as in becoming a one-trick pony, you are more than likely turning one (or more) of the other habits into a rusty mess.

Andre discovered the second demonstration of balance when he realized that the sales force he had created for his software company was locked into using just two habits. On the one hand, half of his sales team was a great group of influencers. They could turn their relational prowess into real business deals. While this group was a great source of new business, they were horrible at keeping it. On the other hand, the other half of his sales team consisted of executers. Customers loved them for the way that they promised what they could deliver and deliver what they promised. Their project management skills solved many problems, even before the customers knew a problem existed. You guessed it. They were great at keeping business, but were horrible at closing the new stuff.

BUILDING ON THE FOUNDATION

These demonstrations of balance shouldn't be surprising. For years, companies like McKinsey and Accenture have been working with organizations to create alignment. When it comes to aligning individuals within the overall system, the Balanced Scorecard provides an organizing approach. The two definitions of balance within Sales Chaos are applicable to the Balanced Scorecard approach.

In the book *Alignment,* Kaplan and Norton explain the Balanced Scorecard as a way to help business leaders categorize the various enterprise value propositions that can contribute to corporate synergies, including:

- Financial synergies
- Customer synergies
- Business process synergies
- Learning and growth synergies

Source: David Norton and Robert Kaplan, *Alignment.* Harvard University Press, 2006.

Note: We said the second group couldn't close. It wasn't a problem with their prospecting. They could find opportunities all the over the place, but they could not connect with potential customers to develop the influence they needed to go past the first round of initial customer conversations (aka the vendor bake-off).

Andre was left with a dilemma. Unfortunately, his advisors were telling him to give his folks presentation skills and sales funnel management training. Either that or start firing folks and hiring new ones. Andre didn't like either choice, but he couldn't articulate the real need either. The problem was not that his folks needed process training or that he needed to start over with new people who would magically "do better." The problem was that they needed balance.

How familiar does this scenario sound to you? Go ahead and change the names or the titles, but you will probably find the second demonstration of balance being ignored all over the place.

CHECKING YOUR BALANCE

MIRROR MOMENT

How's your balance – both demonstrations?

First, how well do you keep your habits within their boundaries? Have you allowed any of them to overextend and become risks? Do you have a reputation as someone people work with, or are you simply someone people work for? Second, how well do you use all of the four habits? Have you allowed any of the habits to get rusty or even disappear?

You may be just one salesperson or you may lead an entire team of salespeople. No matter your role, you must manage both demonstrations of balance. And perhaps the place to start is with your credibility.

CHECKING YOUR CREDIBILITY

Let's go back to the concept of credibility. Have you ever felt the need to sacrifice your credibility to achieve influence, insight, or execution? This is one of the fastest ways to undermine your agility.

As we said earlier, credibility is an enlarger. It makes the impact of your other habits so much stronger. The opposite is also true. Remove credibility, and the other habits basically lose substance and quickly deteriorate.

As the graphic shows, the lack of credibility can release a gigantic minus sign. When your personal effectiveness is taken out of the picture, the other four habits suffer.

Let's start with *influence*. What happens to your influence when you sacrifice your credibility? It literally starts drifting. You can't steer toward anything. Whatever leverage you had built with your influence disappears to the point at which you cannot obtain results through others without dominating them through power. Can you afford to run your business on the basis of power alone? Do you really think the chaos will allow your power to remain unrestricted? No way.

Next, consider *insight*. What happens to your insight when you sacrifice your credibility? At best, you become the master of the obvious. You only discover what folks leave lying around. At worst, your insight grows dark. You know nothing except the information you make up in your head. Know anyone who sells like this?

Finally, look at what happens to *execution* when you sacrifice your credibility. It slows down. It might even stop. The effort you are putting into carrying out your plans will hit obstacle after obstacle. The impact of your full value will become just a fairy tale you tell customers to persuade them to buy from you. Sadly, we see too many salespeople living in this kind of environment, and they want to blame everyone else. We tell those people not to blame the environment until they examine their own credibility.

PAY ATTENTION

When it comes to credibility, here are some things to consider. How well do you?

- Solve problems?
- Embrace diversity?
- Make ethical decisions?
- Manage knowledge?
- Use technology?
- Accelerate your learning?
- Execute plans?
- Maximize personal time?
- Align activity to sales process?

Source: Brian Lambert, Tim Ohai, and Eric Kerkhoff, *World-Class Selling: New Sales Competencies.* ASTD Press, 2009.

Is this making sense to you? We hope so, because without credibility you will not master agility. Ever.

Making It Stick

Take a moment to look at how your credibility is impacting your other habits. Start by writing down three of your most important customers and listing the words Influence, Insight, and Execution next to each customer.

Now, using this list, determine whether balancing your credibility will impact how your customer perceives your other habits. Circle anything that benefits from balancing credibility and quickly write three things you can do to create balanced credibility.

Define any obstacles to your credibility and start eliminating them. If you cannot eliminate the obstacle, determine your plan for minimizing it. Then, start moving forward. Progress, even in small doses, is your ticket to success.

Navigating the Chaos with Agility

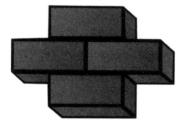

"Habit is either the best of servants or the worst of masters."

Nathaniel Emmons

INTRODUCTION

In Chapter 5, we took a break in order to spend some time wrapping up the concept of sales chaos theory we had discussed in the first four chapters. Here we'll pause briefly to reflect on what we discussed in Chapters 7 through 11.

REVIEW: AGILITY SELLING

As you remember, Chapter 6 provided a brief history of sales methodologies as well as a brief history of Agility Selling. We defined Agility Selling as a non-linear; pattern-based approach to selling with two rules:

1. Instead of focusing on the stages of your sales process, *focus on your selling skills.*
2. Instead of focusing on selling your product or service, *focus on justifying the customer's definition of full value.*

The Two Rules of Agility Selling

Agility Selling is not a sales *technique.* Neither is it a sales *process.* While techniques and processes are valuable, Agility Selling is a broader methodology. It is a genuinely fresh approach to selling, birthed by chaos and grounded in science.

When we use the term "selling skills," we are talking about what you need to know and what you need to do in order to be successful. Selling skills apply to any selling environment: your sales culture, your territory, your customer, etc. More importantly, selling skills allow you co-create solutions with your customer while focusing on driving relevant results and outcomes.

PAY ATTENTION

What you think matters.
What you *do* matters more.
What you do repeatedly will impact your life
   significantly.

In Chapter 7, we introduced the first rule of Agility Selling and began explaining the Four Habits of Agile Sellers. We included a brief definition of sales professionalism as well as the obstacles to skill. We talked about the ways to ensure the impact of the four habits is achieved before going into a deeper overview of each habit.

The Four Habits of Agile Sellers

Remember, the four habits are:

• Influencing others through the power of relationships
• Generating insight by understanding beyond the obvious

- Executing your plan for the full value experience
- Building credibility through personal effectiveness

In Chapter 8, we covered the first habit, influencing others. We explained what we meant by this habit, especially as influence pertains to your customer. Influence gives you the ability to have an effect on people and, ultimately, on results. Influence is not simply the art of relationships. Relationships give you a cup of coffee. Influence gives you the power to move sales conversations forward. To create influence, you must leverage both conformity and motivation.

In Chapter 9, we talked about generating insight. Insight is the secret of understanding beyond the obvious. It is seeing the facts in a fresh and innovative way. (*Hint:* This is what your customers are looking for from you.) Why is insight so vital? With this core habit, we are giving you the jet fuel of decision making. As a sales professional, your job is defined by decisions. To generate insight, you have to remove assumptions and expand perspectives.

In Chapter 10 we talked about executing your plan and the importance of organizing the full value experience. We said that the concept of value is everything that a customer expects in association with the product or service being sold. We also shared that salespeople don't just sell a product or service—they sell an experience. Value management is about developing strategies to generate support for the solution you define. It covers how you discover, position, and deliver your value. And if you think you can manage the full value experience without project management skills, you are clearly not operating with an understanding of what your customers want in today's economy.

In Chapter 11, we wrote about building credibility and how all you do is a demonstration of your personal effectiveness. You discovered how personal effectiveness can help you experience the kind of success you expect with your customers. We also showed you how the habit of credibility can push into the other habits. We gave you two demonstrations of balance. The first is to make sure that the four core habits are used with a healthy sense of boundaries, as in, I influence you, but not too much. I share my insight with you, but not too much. And so on. The second demonstration of balance is to make certain that all four habits are in play. Our research showed that every one of the four habits is vital to your ability to carry out your job.

PAY ATTENTION

Revisit "Keep, Start, Stop" on a daily basis.
 You must decide what you want to keep doing, what you want to stop doing, and what you need to start doing.

Research has also shown that it takes three weeks (around twenty-one days) to make a habit part of your life. Since we call influence, insight, execution, and credibility "habits," it would suggest that you have to ingrain them into your selling approach. More importantly, you must realize that all of your selling skills ultimately rest on the core four habits. What do we mean? We have trained thousands of salespeople and sales managers throughout the world, and they always want to discuss how to create and close opportunities or how to manage accounts. These skills are crucial to selling, but your success in engaging clients rests on the four habits. To take it a step further, the many skills required to sell will be wasted in the pursuit of opportunities without the four habits in place. Listening will be wasted because you'll be listening for the wrong thing. Presentations will miss the point. Questions will be irrelevant. And problem solving won't exist.

How are you doing with living these habits? By reading about the four habits, you may have discovered that you are not as proficient with them as you would like, and that's ok. Or perhaps you discovered that you were pretty good at the four habits a while ago, but now is the time to revisit them or go back to the basics, and that's ok as well. Habit-building can be difficult, but here are some tried-and-true suggestions that can help.

1. *Focus on consistency:* When it comes to the four core habits, consistency is critical. Build them into your daily workflow. For example, add a section of influencing, value management, insight, and personal effectiveness into your account planning

process. To help with consistency, you can also develop a personal learning plan that targets one (or more) habits. You can read books, discuss each habit with clients and customers, or receive coaching advice from your manager.

2. *Don't try to completely change your sales approach in one day.* We have seen many salespeople get excited about the concept of Agility Selling and try to completely change their behavior in one day. This isn't realistic. A better approach would be to target one area of improvement and work on it on a consistent basis for a dedicated length of time. For example, for the next three days really zero in on gaining and sharing insight. Look for new insight. Find ways to leverage technology to share insight. Ask your customers where they gain their insight, and so forth. When it comes to building a habit, think of the concept of dedicated practice. Practice your behavior repeatedly in order to make it a habit.

3. *Don't expect all your attempts to change habits to be successful immediately.* Remember that it took time to learn your old habits too. Set specific goals around each habit and engage your colleagues or management team with a specific request to help ingrain the habits over time. You'd be surprised about the conversations you can have regarding influence, insight, execution, and credibility. Incorporate these habits into your discussions as a way to remind you of their importance.

4. *Re-familiarize yourself with the benefits of making a change.* It's easy to slip back into the old way of doing things. It's like muscle memory in a golf swing. Your body gets used to swinging a golf club in a particular way and builds up muscle memory so that it becomes routine. To get to that point, the best golfers in the world take thousands, if not hundreds of thousands, of golf swings. Once that muscle memory is built up, however, it's difficult to change. Every muscle involved in swinging the golf club (and there are hundreds) must be retrained, and it's never comfortable. What muscle memory do you have around your current habits? What are the benefits of rethinking and revisiting them, building new muscle memory around them? How would these benefits make a difference in the life of your customers?

CONSIDER THIS

Here are some helpful suggestions for changing your behavior:

1. *Write down your goal.* There is magic in the written word. We recommend stating your goal in positive terms, such as "I want to be able to have a successful meeting with a CIO." Begin by writing down your goal and staying positive.

2. *List your reasons for changing or eliminating your habit.* Writing these down forces you to think in specific terms about what the habit represents in your career (for example, "I have a habit of staying within my comfort zone and only meeting with lower-level buyers in the customer's organization"). Writing things down also helps you identify the opportunities you believe your career will hold for you upon changing the habit (for example, "If I don't change my approach to the CIO-level buyer, I won't be able to sell my products or solutions, so I won't be as successful as I could be"). This will also help you commit to taking positive action.

3. *Motivate yourself.* Tell yourself you're making progress. Remind yourself that you are moving closer to your goal. Talk to yourself throughout the day about how you are going to avoid triggers that can take you off track and derail your efforts.

4. *Find alternative approaches.* For example, if you want to have a conversation with a CIO, find a way to practice in a safe environment (for example, role play, find a friend who knows a CIO you can talk to, attend a CIO event).

5. *Enroll others for support.* Explain why you are making this change. Ask for support. Support could be needed encouragement or the person

may be able to help you find new information, new ideas, or new connections.

6. *Be prepared for people who aren't supportive.* Be assertive and tell these people why you are doing what you are doing and that you notice they are not helping your efforts. If you need to take action toward your goal and someone isn't being supportive, be assertive and state your thoughts.

Since we're talking about what it takes to build and reinforce habits, we would like to point out that any time you undertake a personal change, it takes a lot of work. There are no shortcuts or "silver bullets" that will ever make it easier. To effect a change in habits, you have to become aware of the habits and regain the ability to make choices. Choices are what the four habits are all about. Making the right choices now will help you reap rewards later.

You will not master Agility Selling without them.

Making It Stick

Creating a Journal Entry

Take a moment to reflect on what you have been reading. We have used a lot of stories and examples while also relaying a lot of information about habits and principles you need to have to be successful. Before moving on to the next chapter, take a moment and reflect.

Using the space provided, write some notes to yourself.

1. What are your key takeaways from Chapters 6 through 11?

2. Have you identified any areas that you personally want to improve? What are they?

3. Do you know someone who can discuss this with you?

4. In the next ninety days, what are your top two or three priorities?

SECTION
3

Selling Differently, Part Two

Justifying Full Value

"Chaos in the world brings uneasiness, but it also allows the opportunity for creativity and growth."

Tom Barrett

INTRODUCTION

In the previous six chapters, we talked about the first rule of Agility Selling: Instead of focusing on the stages of your sales process, focus on your selling skills. Now we move onto the second rule of Agility Selling: Instead of focusing on selling your product or service, focus on justifying the customer's definition of full value.

WHY FULL VALUE IS IMPORTANT

This concept of the entire bundle of expectations that drive the buyer through discovering, positioning, and delivering value is the key ingredient that makes buyers act like snowflakes. (They're all unique, remember?)

We now want to take our conversation on full value further by focusing on the way to leverage Agility Selling to justify full value. In other words, from the customer's perspective, we will define what the customer needs to see from you, the sales rep.

When it comes to justifying full value, you need to work backwards from the customer. In other words, focus on the fact that you have something that the customer probably expects in order to solve a specific problem—but he or she may not be able to completely define it yet.

Ok, you're thinking . . . but what exactly does that mean? How is it that customers can want more than they are articulating?

We call it the Starbuck's Effect.

The Starbuck's Effect describes how people can unknowingly bundle multiple expectations as part of one simple price in their buying experience. To the customer, purchasing a no foam, non-fat, decaf latte with a half-pump of vanilla is boiler-plated as a single price with a single up-charge for the vanilla, funky music and living room atmosphere included. Just grab your cup and keep moving please.

You see, people are not typically thinking, "Wow. What a great deal I am getting. I can actually change the ingredients of my drink so that my order can change every time I buy, all at one consistent price. Think of all of the logistics that go into sourcing and delivering regular, whole, and skim milk. Plus soy milk. That must take a lot of hard work and planning. I should take a moment and sit in this comfortable chair to ponder it." Yeah, right! Most likely, customers are only thinking about whatever comes to mind. But if you took away their options, imagine what would happen. Not a happy thought.

CONSIDER THIS

Only your customer can define value. You cannot tell your customer what value is. But you can use your Four Habits of Agile Sellers to help your customers agree on the value they need, agree on what value they can actually have, and agree on the impact the value provides. Hey. You just made a snowflake.

The Starbuck's Effect explains why even the most seasoned salespeople are still struggling in today's economy. Even when we work very hard to position our value as a greater solution, customers have been conditioned to expect the products and services we sell to be bundled at no extra cost and that we will include all the other unmentioned extras for free as well. Unless you are fortunate enough to work in an industry that is sitting at the forefront of innovation, your product or service is constantly being treated as just another commodity—with a half-pump of vanilla syrup.

Which is why we keep circling around the concept of full value. Your customers want more than the solution you are selling. They want the entire experience, even if they don't define it clearly, and they will complain when they don't get it. It's the Starbucks Effect in your day-to-day business.

BLENDING EXPECTATIONS AND ALTERNATIVES

Although buyers can bring a lot of expectations to the table, they are not the only one with demands. Everyone involved in the experience has a set of expectations. When you can find out all of the expectations that exist, you can begin to understand how customers will eventually define what they want from their full value experience.

PAY ATTENTION

Although buyers can bring a lot of expectations to the table, they are not the only one with demands. Everyone involved in the experience has a set of expectations.

Think about that for a moment. If you could look ahead to see what the customer will eventually complain about, would that change how you sell? Would you start asking different questions? Would you stop repeating trite old sales slogans? Would you look for all of the unspoken expectations the customer has?

Hear this clearly. It's not *your* expectations that define value. The *buyer's* expectations define value as he or she attempts to solve a problem. Whenever a customer complains about something, it is almost always tied to the expectations of full value he thought he would receive from you. This includes all the stuff tied to your product or service, whether or not there is explicit agreement or not. In other words, you may not have included all the buyer's expectations in your sales materials, but you sold them just the same.

Expectations

This means that, as you understand your customers better, you will realize that the buyer's definition of what is important is tied to all of the expectations being placed on him by his own buying community. You will learn about these expectations within a variety of sales conversations, and you will then begin to see patterns in the problems that he is trying to solve. You will now grasp that this overarching definition of value, this full value, is determined by how you and your company meet – and even exceed – the buying community's expectations.

But here is where is gets tricky. Knowing, understanding, realizing – all of these terms simply mean that you can see the problem. It doesn't actually give you the ability to do something about it. Yet.

Let's add in the next element – justifying the definition of full value.

Those of us in the sales profession have all heard about "communicating value." Unfortunately, communicating value is often overly simplified and presented as a series of conversations about the products and services that you promised in your contract. In other words, "communication" stops for some reason, when the "selling" starts.

We believe that, instead of selling your solution (your product or service), you need to justify the customer's definition of full value as it relates to the problem he or she is trying to solve. This puts the customer's buying and problem-solving processes front and center, so you can identify patterns and work forward from there.

So, instead of trying to force your product or service into your discussions with customers, start by understanding how to define, position, and deliver full value so you can turn the conversation toward justifying what *they* would define as valuable in that moment and–more importantly–throughout the problem-solving and buying processes.

Let's put it another way. If we asked you to define what you sell, what would you tell us? Your answer, right or wrong, would be the cornerstone of how you live as a sales professional. If you told us that you sold tools, your day-to-day activities would be about how you try to find potential customers who need your tools. If you told us that you sold efficiency, your day-to-day activities would be about how you try to find potential customers who need the efficiency your tools provide. And if you told us that you sold better business results, your day-to-day activities would be about how you find potential customers who are looking to turn efficiency into better business outcomes. These answers seem pretty reasonable, don't they?

But what if we said we don't recommend you "sell" anything? What if we said that your customers don't want to be sold anything? Some of you would find that line of reasoning a little hard to swallow, but we'll guess that most of you reading this already know that your customers really only want you to define, position, and deliver full value so they can justify their decisions. If you can't help them do this (let alone understand their problems), they really don't want to talk with you.

MIRROR MOMENT

Here's your first mirror moment of the chapter. Does your day-to-day schedule look more like you are spending your time defining, positioning, and delivering full value for your most important customers or prospects or more like you are trying to just sell them something?

Want to test yourself? Think about how much you complain about wasting your time cleaning up other people's messes.

Seriously. If we had an after-hours conversation with you at your favorite watering hole, how long would it take for you to start complaining about your frustrations with your own company? Five minutes? Fifteen minutes? An hour? The shorter the amount of time (and especially the frequency of the topic) before it appears in your end-of-day chats with colleagues is an indicator of whether or not you just sell value or aggressively justify it.

Face it. If you are just selling value, you are only focused on getting through the close. Your day is one big hunting trip. And heaven forbid that anything gets in the way! In fact, anyone who brings a distraction to this endless pursuit of hunting deals will usually be greeted by scorn and contempt.

But our definition isn't limited to the people who are trying to sell to new customers. Salespeople who are trying to expand their relationships with existing customers can be just as guilty. Consider the salesperson who spends all of her time managing the delivery process. In fact, all of her time is consumed by just taking care of the status quo. If you ask her to tell you how things are going, she will likely tell you a long story of how she is fixing this, following up on that, and maybe even exploring something else. But never creating anything. This person is just as guilty of simply selling her products and services because she only delivers what was sold. She never creates anything new. Her entire definition of what the customer wants is wrapped up in a transaction—at best, one endless cycle of smaller transactions or, at worst, delegation to lower levels in the organization (such as procurement). This person's day looks like a hamster on a wheel. Guess how much value the customer takes away from this salesperson?

On the other hand, imagine this. You have effectively trained your mind to identify the butterflies, you have created enough stability with your anchor points, and you have slowed the chaos enough to actually see the individual snowflakes as they swirl around you. If you are practicing the Four Habits of Agile Sellers (and that is a huge requirement), then you are ready for the conversations that are required for a professional higher-level business interaction and a sustained business relationship.

But at this point, your conversations are still interactions, not tied to any forward momentum. You can talk and talk and talk with the customer community, but what are you going to talk about? This is where justifying your full value comes in.

Justifying full value means you're expanding your sense of responsibility to include any unspoken expectations. It means that you are looking for ways to promote and defend your full value for the host of folks who have something to say about doing business with you and your company—even if you don't have a brochure for it.

Of course, you must be able to deliver against what you promise. And this does not mean that all customer expectations are legitimate. Try as we might, even with the rigors of Six Sigma thinking, there will be errors in the system. But if everyone has the same errors in the system, the customer should change expectations, right? If no one in the world can give the customer what he or she is demanding, doesn't that mean that the customer needs to calm down a bit? Now we are getting to the heart of justifying full value.

Alternatives

Justifying full value pushes you to not only work with the customer's expectations, but to also take charge of the *alternatives* the customer has to address them. It means that you are *blending their expectations and alternatives* to discover, position, and deliver your full value.

For example, a really big customer wants a new reporting capability added to how they manage the inventory they bought from you. They want to track both the quantity and speed that the inventory is being consumed, real time. And they expect that data to be bundled with the monthly invoice so they can see the various inventory levels throughout the month. Nice expectation, but let's calibrate it against the alternatives.

If this is something that can be done, even if it's only being done by your competitors, you have a lot of work ahead of you. But if no one in your industry is able to offer that kind of support, you still have a lot of work ahead of you because you must help that customer see that the expectations are not realistic. But a truly agile, rigidly flexible sales professional will go a step further. He will take some time to figure out whether the expectation can be used to create even more value. Is this just about an inventory report? What is the greater problem to be solved? And if we know the problem, could we create alternatives that change the impact of our full value dramatically?

Now we are going beyond simply knowing what the problem is. We are actively defining what to do next, especially if it helps us create and justify our full value. If we are justifying our full value, the customer will see that we are generating the maximum amount of full value available.

Ready to learn more about this idea? Keep reading.

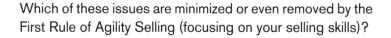

Making It Stick

Go back to the list of challenges you created at the end of Chapter 6. Ask yourself:

Which of these issues are minimized or even removed by the First Rule of Agility Selling (focusing on your selling skills)?

- Why does it change?

- What specifically changes?

- How will you make these changes happen?

- What will you do if the challenge takes more effort than you originally thought?

Finally, keep an eye on the remaining issues as you read the next few chapters on Rule 2. Let's see what goes away next.

The Six Buyer Expectations and How to Manage Them

"Chaos results when the world changes faster than people do."

Anonymous

INTRODUCTION

As we explained in the last chapter, justifying value is much more than managing the transaction cycle. Justifying value is about seeing the entire snowflake experience with the kind of clarity that completely transforms these separate conversations. It is about using the Four Habits of Agile Sellers to discover, position, and deliver value in a way that creates and defends new definitions of value, often in ways that are unrelated to your products or services. It is not ignoring transactions; it is going beyond them to encompass the entire full value experience you create over time with your customer.

Let's finally get into the grittier elements of this concept called "expectations." By now, we all agree that, long before you present a solution, and long after you close the deal, all buyers have expectations. Expectations are constantly shifting throughout the customer's relationship with you. Through your conversations with the buyer, you'll begin to work with the buyer's definition of full value. Those conversations have a series of phases. Many salespeople call that the "sales process" or the "sales cycle." But the traditional linear sales process (especially the sales funnel) is quickly becoming obsolete because the conversations no longer occur in a straight line.

So what happens when you focus on just one expectation of the transaction? Or worse, what happens when you limit the amount of value that you can even discuss? Let's look at Tony's story.

There was once a large financial services company responsible for disbursing retirement funds. Many of the people who were supposed to receive their retirement funds didn't keep their former employers up-to-date on their mailing addresses. There were thousands of people the financial services company had no way to contact. Now imagine what it would be like to be in charge of paying out a huge amount of unclaimed money to people you couldn't find while also having the government constantly looking over your shoulder to make sure things were done efficiently, ethically, and on time. Not fun.

Enter our friend, Tony.

Tony had been pulled into the relationship to help the customer position value, in this case helping the financial services company select a supplier (his company) to deal with their problem. Tony's company provided a useful service by tracking people down so that they could start receiving the unclaimed pension money that was due them. Tony was able to successfully close the deal on the promise that the value the customer received would center on successfully disbursing unclaimed funds and getting the government off their back. He handed the deal over to the contracts team to formalize the agreement and confirm expectations. Then the dynamics of delivering value took over. That's when the trouble started.

The first issue was over the concept of "three months." Tony had accurately told the customer that it would take three months to find the missing people. What had not been said was that the three months started when the IT support group received the list of names so that they could start generating data reports to begin the tracking process. The customer had assumed that it was three months from when the contract was signed. Never mind that it took a month to give the names to the supplier. When a month had gone by since the contract was signed, the customer called Tony's call center for a status report. Nothing had been done yet (they had just received the names). The customer was not happy.

The call center manager was upset at Tony for not managing expectations properly, even though it wasn't Tony's responsibility to have managed that bit of information. Tony had to go back and re-position the value to address this gap. Tony, seeing how expectations had not been properly managed, took full responsibility for the gap on himself and promised to deliver the value his customer was paying for. Unfortunately, it just grew worse from there.

The operations folks fell behind on delivery. Then account services could not correctly bill the customer (they duplicated invoices, entered incorrect pricing, and even entered incomplete orders). By the time Tony was brought back in (no one had thought to send him an email telling him of the problems as they actually occurred), the list of things he had to go back to the customer and explain was almost unbearable. Even so, Tony went back to the customer to re-position his value yet again. Which he was successfully able to do. Barely.

Tony recognized that he had to get things back on track to make sure his customer received the full value he had promised. Tony recognized that he was the only one trying to keep track of all of the customer's expectations. The various departments had fallen into the trap of focusing on just one expectation at a time. Tony decided that he needed to talk to someone who could help the internal groups think differently, which meant he had to talk to his CEO.

When he approached the CEO about the problems he was experiencing, Tony was thanked for bringing up this conflict, but he was told to leave it alone. The company would handle things if Tony could just let them work out the kinks.

Say what? The solution was to make sure that the status quo was protected and that no single person had the same definition of full value? Talk about creating your own chaos.

Then, while Tony was picking his jaw off the floor, the CEO actually asked Tony to try and get more business from the customer the next time he visited them. Tony couldn't believe his ears.

Did you see how the concept of full value in this story was limited because people could not, or would not, focus on more than one expectation at a time? There obviously were customer expectations, but there were at least as many internal expectations as well, weren't there? Client services expected operations to keep the timeline intact. Finance expected account services to bill the customer correctly. And Tony expected everyone to at least keep him informed.

Remember, you don't just sell a product or service; you actually sell a positive experience. Since the very definition of full value is provided by the customer, it will shift depending on where in the full value experience your customer is at any given moment. What is valuable during discovery will not be valuable during delivery, and so on (remember Chapter 4). Limiting your focus to a single expectation in any given moment will only limit the amount of full value you can give. And after spending all that effort identifying butterflies, tying into anchor points, and slowing down snowflakes, why would you want to limit the full value you can give?

The challenge is being able to organize the customer's full value expectations in a way that regularly makes sense. In fact, wouldn't it be nice if full value actually had a structure that helped you define it?

PAY ATTENTION

We are giving you a pair of special snow goggles. Use them wisely. The snow goggles have two lenses. One lens is the lens of expectations. The other is the lens of alternatives. You need both to study the customers' snowflakes and identify patterns in the world around you.

For that we need to give you a special pair of glasses. These are the kind of glasses that let you look at snowflakes as they fall and analyze the crystals within them. With this kind of clarity and focus, you have an advantage that your competition most likely doesn't have.

We like to call them snow goggles, because they help you pinpoint and study individual snowflakes in the chaos around you. Snow goggles have two lenses. Each provides a unique perspective on every conversation and moves you that much closer to generating revenue. Although these lenses are twins, they are not identical. Think of them as fraternal twins. Close enough to complete each other's thoughts but different enough to easily tell them apart.

The first lens is called the Lens of Expectations. The second lens is called the Lens of Alternatives. For now, we are going to spend our time on the Lens of Expectations. Don't worry, we will explain all about the Lens of Alternatives in the next chapter.

CONSIDER THIS

Have you ever stopped to categorize the expectations your customers have? We're willing to bet you haven't. As a key element of the Agility Selling methodology, we encourage you to spend some time thinking about what their expectations look like so you'll have a firm foundation for justifying full value.

THE SIX EXPECTATIONS

We have found that the expectations of full value can be organized into six categories. Each of these is related to one of the expectations that your customers can have. The customer defines them. You will have to use your four habits to make them work for you.

The six expectations that determine how customers define full value are:

- Satisfaction
- Cost
- Appeal
- Quality
- Efficiency
- Accountability

Anyone who buys from you is expecting all six of these to one degree or another, even if you didn't go over them specifically. Chances are that, if you have to negotiate or overcome an obstacle, it will be because of one or more of these expectations. Additionally, if you're hearing a complaint from one of your customers, it's stemming from your inability to meet one (or more) of these expectations.

While these six expectations can appear in any order and be of varying degrees of importance, they form a pattern. By identifying the customer's expectations, you'll be able to stay on top of the full value experience. In other words, fewer surprises!

Let's unpack these expectations.

Satisfaction

The first expectation is *satisfaction*, that sense of contentment that customers are constantly measuring you against. One could argue that satisfaction is the prime expectation and that all the others are secondary. We wouldn't disagree about the importance of satisfaction, but it's not as simple as rating one over the other. (Remember, we're looking for patterns, no matter how frequent.)

For starters, satisfaction is not rational. It's based on emotions. Satisfaction can be found in that movie everyone was buzzing about that had great special effects, cinematography, and acting, yet you simply weren't satisfied with it when you finally got around to seeing it. In fact, when it won movie of the year, you were left scratching your head. For you, something intangible was missing.

Satisfaction can also be found in the customer who says, "I like doing business with you because I like you." Like? Seriously? Yes, very seriously. The old mantra is true: People do business with the people they like.

The key is to recognize that satisfaction is a legitimate business energy you have to manage and account for. If you don't, it will turn into a butterfly (a very vocal, very unhappy customer).

So ask yourself: Do you justify satisfaction? If you do, you look for ways to create satisfaction – and work to get credit for it when you do. It may be the most important part of your value offering. But before we go too far down that path, let us give you five more ways to look at full value.

Cost

The second expectation is *cost*. Cost is different than price. The price is just a snapshot of what someone paid today. If you haven't learned by now, people see economic factors in terms that are bigger than sticker price, as in, "What will it cost me to buy your product or service?" There's the up-front cost, and the hidden cost, and the ongoing cost, and so on. There are almost too many to count. Therefore, our definition of cost is *the entire economic investment over time*.

And trust us. Your value, from this perspective, will change over time. Sometimes, customers will think that the value they received for what they paid is fantastic. Other times, you will get the exact opposite opinion. And it can all happen with a single deal.

The key is to check your customers' perception of cost. Even if they paid for your solution months ago, justifying the full value means that you are looking for ways to make the next economic decision an easier one for them.

Appeal

The third expectation is *appeal*. Appeal is found through the logical match of your total portfolio against the customer's senses. Yes, appearance matters. So do smell, and feel, and the rest of the senses. There is quite of bit of science behind the expectation of appeal.

Here is an example. Tim is a big guy. You can sell Tim a seat on your airline, but if the seats are uncomfortable he will likely not fly with you again. It's just simple body mechanics. And the converse is true. He will pay more for a seat on an airline that has enough space to keep his knees from being bashed by the innocent traveler in front of him.

Quality

The fourth expectation is *quality*. Practically speaking, this refers to the reliability your customers expect from you, especially in terms of the products or services you communicate about and then deliver effectively. If you sell something that breaks or doesn't work as promised, it will affect the buyer's other expectations. For example, it won't really matter how low the cost was or how inviting the appeal was. If your solution is not deemed to be reliable, you risk your credibility.

Since you probably don't run your own manufacturing or services division, the key is to stay on top of your customer's perception of reliability. You must then communicate that expectation to important internal team members. Look for ways to reinforce the customer's expectation of quality, especially when things go right. Take ownership of your quality message, and marshal internal resources when things go wrong. Better yet, use the Agility Selling methodology to identify the problem before it occurs and address it before it affects your reputation.

Efficiency

The fifth expectation is *efficiency*. Simply put, efficiency is all about your customer's perception of speed. Speed matters. How long does it take to start on initiatives, finish a task, or fix a problem? How long does it take you to accomplish the same thing with equal or greater effectiveness? Even if the problem lies with some internal department, your customer will remember your face and phone number.

The key to managing the efficiency expectation is being able to calibrate what your customer expects. Bring your own assessment of how fast you and your company can be into the discussion first. Be accurate, not overly optimistic. You should know where your company is most efficient and where it is not. Then you can influence the customer's expectations toward the most realistic definition of efficiency. Feel free to beat those expectations later.

PAY ATTENTION

Be careful not to equate efficiency with effectiveness. They are very different. Effectiveness is part of the expectation of quality. When customers are motivated by effectiveness, they are expecting quality. Of course, customers usually expect both at the same time. Giving them a quick answer that is not reliable will never be greeted positively. Neither will a reliable response that comes too late.

Accountability

The sixth, and perhaps the most important, expectation is *accountability*. Accountability is how your customer perceives your ownership of the full value experience. Are you accountable for satisfaction, cost, benefit, quality, and efficiency? Are you taking responsibility to ensure that the value promised is the full value delivered?

Having your customer recognize that you are accountable for your actions and the actions of your company is the bedrock of building a loyal customer. You've likely seen the research that proves over and over again: Sellers who help customers solve their problems successfully create more loyal customers than those who ignore customer problems or don't uncover them in the first place. Why? Because accountability really matters to buyers.

Sadly, too many people want to skirt accountability these days. How often do you hear about someone who takes full responsibility for a customer's bad experience? Not often enough. In fact, we are more likely to see people pointing fingers at somebody else down the value chain.

Whether you are in a position of authority or not, your customers want to know they can trust you. They will accept mistakes as long as there is someone to own them. Take that ownership. Understand what accountability means to your customer and how you can take action. You will likely have to work internally to find people who will share responsibility with you. And you will have to help them understand what your customer has already told you.

MANAGING BUYER EXPECTATIONS

Six expectations, six opportunities to justify value. Or lose it. Together they make up the lens of expectations, and fully leveraging the Agility Selling methodology means that you shift your focus from trying to sell your products and services to creating and defending the kind of full value your customers want.

CONSIDER THIS

Try to have a conversation about solving a customer's problem without talking about your product or service. Have a colleague role play the customer, and ask him or her to let you know when you bring up your company or your product or service. You may find this extremely difficult. Typically, when we run this exercise, within four minutes the salesperson has (a) run out of stuff to talk about or (b) fallen into the trap of pushing the product or service he or she offers!

Imagine how agile you would be if you managed expectations instead of services or products. For instance, think about how the conversation would shift if you saw customer issues through their expectations of accountability. How would the actual content of your conversation change? How would you ask questions differently? We're not saying that you should throw accountability around whenever you have the chance. You should only seek to understand the expectations your customer has, and then communicate with your customer very clearly when he or she surfaces one of those expectations. We want you to think about how your conversation might shift and plan for it accordingly. Use open-ended questions to explore each expectation to see whether a defined need exists.

Frankly, you may be guilty of breaking one of the cardinal rules of sales: If there's no defined need, there is no value.

Look at late-night infomercials for knives. Do I need to cut a radish into a red, red rose? Do I need to cut my shoe in half? Do I need to bend a knife sideways? While those "needs" are entertaining, we can't think of a logical reason to bring that kind of thinking into modern, professional selling.

It is amazing to us how often salespeople don't understand the principle of defined need. Have you ever had to sit through a sales presentation where you are being bombarded by an endless list of features and explanations that have nothing to do with your actual needs, even while you think, "When is this going to be over?" Or worse, have you ever made one of your own customers go through this kind of torture?

The principle of defined need asserts that, until the customer has told you a need exists and that he expects it to be addressed, you cannot assume that he will buy anything. This means that you must constantly look at what your customer is expecting. That is not to say that you can't bring up other expectations during the conversation. Obviously, you should explore and manage all six expectations at least once to see whether any is of importance. Just do it in a way that the customer can appreciate.

The human brain can process an amazing amount of information during any given second, but it only allows a limited amount of that information to sit in the front row seat we call "consciousness" (usually about seven chunks). When you have tapped into one expectation, stay there until the customer has clearly defined the need, then move on to another expectation. Keep the flow of the conversation moving at a pace the customer appreciates – and be intentional. No more stumbling into customer needs accidentally. We've given you a road-map with six checkpoints. Explore them in any order, but explore them nonetheless.

ASSESSING YOUR ABILITY TO MANAGE EXPECTATIONS

After you have explored the six expectations with your customer, evaluate the impact of your involvement. Did you create value or not? Every expectation you successfully address adds to the impact of your full value. Read that again. Every expectation you successfully address adds to the impact of your full value.

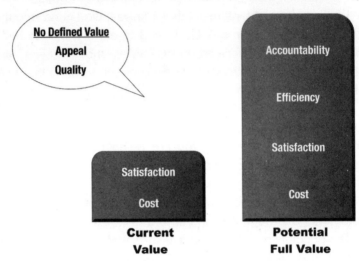

No Defined Value
Appeal
Quality

Accountability

Efficiency

Satisfaction

Satisfaction

Cost

Cost

**Current
Value**

**Potential
Full Value**

Look at the graphic above. The first column shows the customer's current definition of value. In practical terms, this could be the main reason why a customer is not interested in talking with you about switching suppliers. This potential customer is saying, "I like my current supplier and I am happy with my pricing." If you are properly managing expectations, you will use your Four Habits of Agile Sellers to help the customer to define more expectations than just satisfaction and cost. By defining your full value in a way that the customer agrees with, you can help the customer examine other expectations. In this example, the customer defined the additional expectations of efficiency and accountability.

Even if you have no idea what you're doing, and you stumble across value, it matters. That's right, look for ways that your customer wants to give you and your company credit for addressing a need. This can take the form of tactical needs, emotional wants, business demands, professional requirements — whatever.

Remember, expectations do not always have to be logical. Do not limit your conversations to the things that are related to the products and services you have in your portfolio. You can create value, and therefore justify full value, with almost anything – as long as it's important to the customer (that is, one of his or her expectations).

But caution. If the customer will not define an expectation, even if *you* see a clear need, you may not turn that expectation into the full value you are trying to justify. In the graphic, we kept appeal and quality out of the full value. This doesn't mean that the potential customer would not expect these elements in the future. Rather, it means that the customer is not expecting them at this time. Remember, if there is not a defined need, there is no value – at least for now.

Here is where it really is fun. If you can remember the six expectations, you will start to create new ways of pulling them together. You will stop limiting your focus to managing one expectation at a time. You will use the lens of expectations to see every possibility. *Cost* will shift from negotiating payment and credit terms to a discussion about long-term investments and risk management. *Efficiency* will shift from explaining delivery dates to helping customers beat their own time demands and the impact that has on their own operations. Really, the possibilities are endless. It will all depend on the business you are in, where you are in the value experience, and who you are talking with. In other words, understanding the six expectations will help you steer just about any conversation to a place where value can be justified.

Need to get the customer to share his or her needs? Use the lens of expectations as a way to start the conversation, then adjust the dialogue based on the expectations of the person you are talking with. Need to separate yourself from the competition? Steer clear from selling your products and services and start talking about the full value that is important to the customer, based on all of the expectations he or she has. You may have cost and quality similar to other suppliers, but you should have at least one other expectation you can use as a differentiator. Remember, it's about the customer's expectations. If the customer genuinely does not have expectations for appeal, quit trying to push it into the conversation. If you find yourself in a meeting with two people and one decision-maker is keen on cost, but the other is focused on quality, don't push cost on the quality buyer and quality on the cost buyer. In other words, justify what actually exists, not the value you wish was there. Just as Cameron did.

Cameron was responsible for selling customer relationship management (CRM) software to large companies. Selling to other sellers is a tough gig because salespeople can be some of the most skeptical buyers. But Cameron had a high-quality solution that he confidently felt could outperform any other competitor in the market. There was only one problem. It was new. No one really knew what his CRM solution could do. At this time, Cameron was trying to sell his CRM software to the national headquarters of a multinational consumer products company. The company needed to upgrade from its current solution, mainly because their own sales force refused to use it because it was too "clunky." When they met with Cameron, they were skeptical about the strength of a new product and weren't sure whether the new solution would really meet their needs.

Pause. Put yourself in Cameron's place. What thoughts are coming to your mind? Are you already thinking about *how* you want to sell? DON'T. Slow yourself down. Agility Selling demands that you slow your thinking down to identify the full value first. You need to think this through, and you need to be more disciplined. Your first thought should be: "What questions do I have?" You had better have lots of them. Do not let a gap in influence, insight, execution, or credibility become a butterfly now.

MIRROR MOMENT

This brings us to a mirror moment. How often do you do that? Jump ahead in your thinking, that is. Are you so used to hearing the same answers from customers that you have lost your curiosity?

You will never understand your customers' expectations without a healthy sense of curiosity. Curiosity will keep you focused on your habits and help you explore more than one facet of value, which you will need to do when you secure agreements with the customer—and justify your full value.

Ok. Back to Cameron.

During his initial two meetings, Cameron used the lens of expectations to gain a sense of the customer's needs. If you haven't guessed already, they were appeal (the sales force had to like the interface), cost (which has a funny way of almost always showing up), and quality. Great, Cameron thought. He had three of the six uncovered, and he had an answer for each of them. The problem? So did his competition. His biggest competitor was a big-name supplier who was chomping at the bit for this piece of business. To make matters tougher, Cameron did not have previous clients and customers who could rave about his solution (satisfaction). Fortunately for him, the other supplier had eroded their brand strength with rumors of haphazard implementations. This meant that Cameron could separate from his competition with the right play. In this case, it wasn't satisfaction. It was accountability. Cameron could (and did) promise to guarantee every aspect of the full value he was trying to justify. He thought ahead to the delivery phase and built a business case to clearly articulate the resources and training he would provide, the service level the buyer could expect, and even the projected implementation timeline. Then he offered dedicated technical support (with his manager's approval, which he had to fight for) in case the customer experienced any snags with the CRM. This immediately got the complete attention of the customer.

You see, while it had not been stated up-front, the buyers in this scenario were really concerned with risk—the risk of making a mistake. Cameron did not find out until later that one of the key decision-makers had been the person who formalized the purchase of the original solution. While the executive team overseeing sales had initially been delighted to bring such a big-name brand to support the sales force, it had become a very unpleasant topic as folks started talking about the "waste of money" their current CRM system had become.

The key was this: Cameron made justifying the full value his priority from the very beginning. He did not walk in and look for a couple of needs that he could position his CRM product against. That's what his competitor did. Cameron looked for every possible definition of value that the customer had, then did his best to define the impact of his full value. The result was that he had the strongest offer, and he did it much more quickly than if he had waited for needs to appear on their own.

Pause. Do you do that? Do you wait for needs to appear? In more painful terms, how often do new needs appear during your negotiations? While you can likely find something new at any point in the full value experience, you should not make it a habit to be hit by unexpected needs or what are commonly called "objections." If this describes you, you are not justifying full value. You are selling a product or service. And you need to stop. If you think you need to handle objections better, you are mistaken. You must understand the customer's expectations better. Use your four habits to create and defend the full value that the buyer's expectations define.

This is how Cameron closed his deal. When the customer saw that he was serious about backing up his claims, they gave him a trial run with a sampling of their own salespeople. The sales force loved the new CRM. It was easy to operate and easy to look at (appeal). It allowed folks the chance to accurately track their most important customers (quality) while providing the executive team a clear snapshot into what was happening with the their top-customer portfolio on any given day (quality, with a dose of efficiency), all at a reasonable price (cost). And that accountability panic button Cameron had given to the customer? It never was pushed.

Are you starting to see what we mean by selling differently? We are talking not only about the four habits bringing new life into how you engage the customer, but about enabling you to use the lens of expectations. This lens helps you to shift your focus from products and services to the impact of meeting expectations for satisfaction, cost, appeal, quality, efficiency, and accountability, in other words, justifying full value, not dumping everything out on the table in front of the customer and hoping he will like what he sees.

We hope that you can see how these principles can help you be more agile with customers. Just the simple act of combining the strength of your four habits with the power of finding the customer's six expectations of full value will make you more effective.

If the new world of selling were simply about the buyer's expectations, you wouldn't be getting much in the way of new thinking. In fact, if it were only about those expectations, we might have just made your world worse.

You know what worse looks like, don't you? Worse looks like a disgruntled sales force, frustrated with their own company's lack of ability to justify full value and dreading every Monday back on the job. Worse looks like creating unreasonable customer demands and battling continuously, if unsuccessfully, to meet them. Worse looks like taking a growing storm of chaos, surrounded by butterflies and swirling in snowflakes, and turning the chaos factor up by about fifteen notches.

We are not into the idea of worse.

Remember, we told you that justifying your value was about having two lenses. This chapter was about the lens of expectations. Let's go to the next chapter to learn about the second lens, the lens of accountability.

Making It Stick

Think of a current customer. Using the lens of expectations, define every aspect of the full value that customer is expecting. Once you have the broad categories, think through the various ways that the expectation can be expressed. Write them down.

For example, the category of accountability may be a warranty program that you offer, the access your customer wants to your most senior leaders, or even the simple offer that you will personally handle any problems. Chances are that the customer will have more than one way to define each expectation. Are you giving him or her the opportunity to do that?

CHAPTER

The Six Alternatives and How to Leverage Them

"Failure to change is a vice."

Hiroshi Okuda

INTRODUCTION

In 1979, Harvard began the Harvard Negotiation Project to improve the theory, teaching, and practice of negotiation and dispute resolution. This project launched a whole new field – the science of negotiating.

Since then, the research and body of knowledge on negotiating have continued to grow. But we do not want to create another book on the science of negotiating. We want to pull a concept from the research and blend it into how you justify your full value.

207

BUILDING ON THE FOUNDATION

In *Getting to Yes*, Fisher and Ury (1981) presented four key principles: (1) separate the people from the problem; (2) focus on interests rather than positions; (3) generate a variety of options before settling on an agreement; and (4) insist that the agreement be based on objective criteria.

These principles have been proven over and over again, from local business deals to international political treaties. All sales professionals should have a through understanding of how these principles apply to their negotiations.

NEGOTIATION

In 1981, two of the main researchers at the Harvard Negotiation Project, Roger Fisher and William Ury, produced the business classic *Getting to Yes*. In that book, they outlined a new approach to negotiating called principled negotiation. Think of it as the concept of win-win on super-vitamins – academic super-vitamins.

One of the original cornerstones of principled negotiation is called the "best alternative to a negotiated agreement" (BATNA). The theory is to quantify all of the potential impacts that could occur if no agreement were negotiated. It is not the definition of the walk-away point in the negotiation but rather what will most likely happen if no agreement is made. This understanding gives the negotiator a sense of where the leverage is.

In other words, if my BATNA is stronger than the other party's BATNA, I have more leverage in the negotiation. If my BATNA is weaker than the other party's BATNA, the other party has the leverage. If both of our BATNAs are weak, we had better get a deal sorted – and soon.

We take this concept a few steps further and apply it to more than just the negotiated deal. We simply call it the *lens of alternatives*, and we apply alternatives to literally every aspect of the snowflake. In other words, if expectations could pop up, you can bet that alternatives will pop up, too.

> ## CONSIDER THIS
>
> Most sales training is focused on product knowledge, selling skills, competitive knowledge, and company-specific knowledge, like expense reports. But think about it. How much sales training have you had about your customers? For example, how much training have you had on the issues, problems, and challenges your buyers most likely face in their day-to-day jobs? Not enough, we're willing to bet. You have to take your education seriously—be sure *you* own the definition of buyer success, not your competitor.

The sad bit is that most of what is out there in the world of sales training content was developed before Fisher and Ury's idea could be included in how to sell. This omission—or, as we like to call it, this complete failure—has made your job harder than it needs to be. In fact, all of the communication skills and objection-handling training you have had to go through has been pretty anemic without an understanding of alternatives.

Let's explore alternatives a bit more.

BUYERS' ALTERNATIVES

Just as there are six expectations, there are six alternatives but alternatives are broken into two groups: buyers' alternatives and sellers' alternatives.

Generally speaking, every buyer has three alternatives:

- Remain with the "status quo"
- Choose to "do-it-yourself"
- Decide to "find someone" to help

To remain with the status quo means that the buyer will keep things as they already are. The buyer is happy with the value he currently has. Sometimes, good enough really is good enough or sometimes the current value is better than the value being offered. Think about a buyer who will not change suppliers.

For "status quo" to be the best alternative, all other alternatives must not be able to match up against the current situation. Typically, buyers will state that they are happy with the status quo, especially when you only address one expectation. For example, a salesperson can offer a better price, thinking that he is offering a better cost. But what if the customer is already receiving the benefit of volume rebates, fee waivers, or even business development funds. Unless the seller can beat the total status quo cost, the buyer will not budge. In a situation like this, the seller should at least do his homework to find out what other expectations can be addressed to find other alternatives that push status quo off the table.

The buyer's second alternative is to choose to "do-it-yourself." This means the buyer will use her resources and build her own solution. In our personal lives, changing our own motor oil or doing our own home improvements describe this alternative. In business, producing products under a private label is a classic example. Think of the buyer who will agree with the seller that a problem must be addressed and who then works out her own solution to the problem.

For "do-it-yourself" to be the best alternative, all other alternatives must be inferior. This concept is actually more difficult to define. Cost is usually a major element of the buying decision, but so are other expectations. The difficulty with determining whether do-it-yourself is the best alternative is that the buyer must clearly define every expectation.

Well, some expectations are difficult to quantify. How much is efficiency worth? Appeal? Satisfaction? Furthermore, do the buyer's definition and the seller's definition match? A seller trying to maneuver around the do-it-yourself alternative has to be sure that the buyer uses the same definition of impact that the seller is using. In other words, what the seller thinks efficiency is worth should be almost identical to what the buyer thinks efficiency is worth. If the seller cannot get the buyer to define expectations in the same way that he does, there isn't going to be much room to justify full value.

The buyer's third alternative is to decide to "find someone" to help with the problem. Hire that contractor. Pay that supplier. The thrust behind choosing this alternative is the buyer's recognition that the other two alternatives are less attractive. This is the basis of the traditional sales relationship.

Obviously, the alternative of "finding someone" opens the conversation considerably. The buyer can now entertain a wide variety of offers from multiple sources. This search is eventually limited to two or three options. The buyer, if she has done her homework, will try to find a couple of suppliers who can legitimately compete for the business. The seller in this case must focus on not only providing the best alternative to status quo and do-it-yourself, but must also present himself as the best version of "finding someone" else.

PAY ATTENTION

Alternatives are intricately connected to expectations. When you identify expectations, make sure you take the time to think through each of the alternatives.

Let's focus a little more on the buyer's perspective. If the expectation of cost is your initial driver as a buyer, you must look at status quo, do-it-yourself, and find someone. Let's take a look at how this cost expectation might look if you were purchasing a plane ticket to an exotic island vacation.

Obviously, the alternative of status quo is not desirable because, even though staying home is the cheapest option, you actually want to go to the exotic destination by plane. And just as obviously, unless you want to fly your own plane, the alternative of do-it-yourself is not realistic. As a buyer, you are left with the alternative of finding someone to help you acquire the plane ticket.

To really demonstrate the power of alternatives, you must compare all three. Which buying alternative is most desirable in this scenario? Let's first eliminate do-it-yourself as unrealistic. The chances of you figuring out your own transportation to an exotic island are extremely small. You would then assume that finding someone is the better choice. But that depends. What if the price on the ticket is too high? You will compare the cost of finding someone against your next-best alternative, status quo. In other words, if the price for finding someone is far out of range for you, you will just stay home (or wait until prices come down). So, although we may have initially thought status quo was undesirable, it is vital to defining where the deal will end. Make sense?

SELLERS' ALTERNATIVES

This leads us to the group of seller alternatives. Generally speaking, you have three alternatives for any given opportunity:

- Reach "no agreement"
- Choose to sell to "someone else"
- "Close" the opportunity

Your first alternative is to reach "no agreement." This roughly translates into empty hands and an even emptier bank account.

Candidly, most salespeople avoid this alternative even when they shouldn't. What we mean is that many salespeople will pursue business with the intent to avoid the alternative of no agreement. But what if no agreement is a better alternative than the other choices? If you haven't done this kind of analysis with the lens of alternatives, how will you know when you are making a mistake? Instinct? Please say no. Guessing at which deals are good and which deals are bad will only get you into a lot of trouble.

Your second alternative is to choose to sell to "someone else." This means that you have to identify another person or even another organization to sell to. Maybe it's more work, maybe it's not. If your relationship with another buyer is already in place and the value of achieving that deal is potentially superior to the value of the other deal you are working on, it is not as painful as one might think to walk away from the current conversation. If it beats the first seller alternative we just described, you should be ready to embrace it. But more on that later.

Your third alternative is to "close" the opportunity. Closing refers to the final agreement that can be made when the buyer chooses to "find someone" and that someone is you. But closing the opportunity can also refer to other parts of the value experience. Being selected for the short list of potential suppliers is a close that can occur in the discover value phase. And acquiring responsibility for managing the implementation of a solution during deliver value is also an example of this alternative in action.

But wait. Closing, as some of you know, is not always a positive. Have you ever closed a deal that you eventually regretted? We know. Lemon juice on a paper cut. The point is that, while you have all three alternatives in any given deal, they will not all have the same worth.

Using our earlier analogy of buying a plane ticket for an island vacation, it is easy to see the importance of the seller's alternatives at work. Remember, the buyer's primary expectation is cost. Imagine that you are now the seller. "No deal" is likely not desirable. You want people to pay for your transportation services. You might automatically think that closing is the best alternative, but what if the buyer is not willing or able to accept the cost that you are offering? As the seller, it may actually be easier to find someone else to pay for a seat on the plane to the exotic island vacation. After all, exotic islands are popular destinations. Furthermore, if you have to sell a ticket for too low a cost, you will not be able to cover all of your associated expenses. Remember the Australia deal? While you may have thought that closing was the best alternative, you can see that the impact of each alternative can quickly shift your perceptions.

USING ALTERNATIVES

Chances are, you already knew the six alternatives. They are not rocket science, after all. But do you intentionally use them? When you hear an expectation from a potential buyer, do you filter through the alternatives? And not just the buyer's alternatives, but yours as well? Knowing something and doing something about it are two completely different things. You must apply your knowledge of alternatives over and over again throughout the full value experience. Even when you are not negotiating a final deal, there are plenty of times when you can use the various alternatives to keep the momentum of the sale going. Let's talk about how to do that.

Start by identifying the impacts of both sides' alternatives. Ask yourself, "If the buyer stays with the status quo, what will happen?" "What is the best-case scenario for the buyer? What is the worst-case scenario for the buyer?" Use the same process to evaluate all three of the buyer's alternatives. But don't stop there. Evaluate the impact of your own alternatives. Go through the best/worst case definition of each of your own alternatives. Evaluating the impact on you of the buyer's alternatives (which include finding someone other than you) will quickly show you how desirable your offer is to the buyer and also help you see how much you should be willing to offer to the buyer.

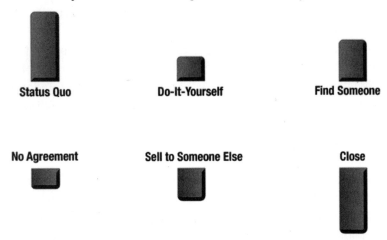

Status Quo   **Do-It-Yourself**   **Find Someone**

No Agreement   **Sell to Someone Else**   **Close**

Look at the graphic. Each bar represents the potential full value that can be achieved with each alternative. From the buyer's perspective, the greatest amount of potential value lies with the alternative of status quo. From the seller's perspective, the greatest amount of potential value lies with closing. What can you learn from this scenario?

First, the buyer has the leverage. From where she is sitting, the status quo doesn't look too bad. The seller is going to have to work hard to acquire this piece of business. Second, the only real value for the seller lies with closing this deal. Neither of the other two alternatives has much potential. Third, and most importantly, the seller has a fairly strong sense of how much to offer the buyer to overcome the pull of the status quo. If the seller cannot increase the full value of finding someone, there will not be anything to justify. No sale will occur.

Pause. Do you purposefully think through how much you are going to offer the buyer? Or do you just throw everything in at one time to see whether the customer bites? This is a dangerous routine. First, you may be giving too much. You may be removing any profit from the deal and causing your company to operate at a loss. Second, you are likely devaluing your offer. The customer will think that the things you are offering are really not that important to you, even if you never intended to give that message. Third, you may be giving the wrong stuff. If you understand the impact of expectations, you will develop a pretty good sense of what the customer finds valuable. That should become the foundation of what you offer. Not the stuff you think is important. The *customer* defines full value, right?

Back to using alternatives.

PAY ATTENTION

After you have a sense of what to offer, keep using the lens of alternatives to track how the deal is developing.

UNEXPECTED ALTERNATIVES

The last thing you want is for an alternative to pop up out of nowhere. This is what Nick learned.

Nick sold medical equipment to hospitals. In one particular instance, he was targeting a hospital he had never been able to work with. He decided to start with helping them discover value. He used his Four Habits of Agility Sellers to set up a conversation with the head of the department that would use his equipment the most.

When the conversation started, it was pretty obvious that the person thought he had no need for Nick's offering. The alternative of status quo was alive and well. Nick knew that if he was going open up the conversation, he needed the customer to recognize the alternative of finding someone. Nick began to probe the current needs and obstacles the hospital was facing and discovered that the time it took to prep a patient for one of the exams was too long. This was creating a problem for the department, as the testing schedule was being overbooked. The doctors were complaining that they couldn't treat their patients fast enough.

Bingo.

Now, instead of just jumping in with his sales pitch, Nick took the time to help the department head recognize all of his expectations, even the ones he initially ignored. Nick asked questions, developing his insight about the impact of the status quo and analyzing the health of the opportunity from his company's perspective. Satisfied with what he saw, he then suggested that the hospital look at options for addressing the problem before it became bigger. The department head agreed, and only then did Nick present one of his products as a potential solution. As far as the buyer was concerned, finding someone was now a legitimate alternative. And for Nick, closing became the best alternative. Nick was now justifying his full value.

Fast-forward a month. At this point, Nick had been able to get the department head to agree that a solution was needed and that Nick's company was a viable option. Nick was now trying to make sure that the alternatives of finding someone and closing were matched up, but there was a problem—price.

Nick started thinking through how he could approach the issue of price. On one hand, he could just lower his price, but he hated that kind of single-expectation, value-limited thinking. So he started going over the various impacts of the buyer's alternatives. The potential impact of status quo on the buyer was pretty negative, but Nick had to help the customer define what that meant. The hospital also had the alternative of do-it-yourself. Nick had seen another hospital deal with a similar problem on its own, and the positive impact of that do-it-yourself approach was so small for that customer that Nick thought he could use that experience to help this hospital avoid a similar mistake. This led Nick to evaluating the buyer's alternative of finding someone else. As far as he could tell, he was the only one running in the race. The current supplier never came around and no one else had quite the solution Nick was offering.

What do you think he was supposed to do next?

If you guessed that he had to get the department head to define the negative impact of status quo, you are correct. Without the impact of this alternative clearly articulated by the customer, Nick couldn't get a sense of which alternative was the best one for the customer. Without a sense of where his customer was in the buying and problem-solving process, Nick couldn't even get a sense of what his own alternatives were. How could he determine whether his best alternative was closing if he had no idea what it would really take to close? Nick was losing the leverage he had created while discovering value, and without any new leverage in positioning value, he couldn't create momentum to advance the conversation beyond price.

Fast-forward two months. Using data Nick had been able to collect from the doctors he talked to, the department head eventually agreed to quantify the impact of a congested testing schedule in real dollars (the loss of testing income, patient and doctor dissatisfaction, and having a poor reputation for that department of the hospital). With the impact of the buyer's alternative agreed upon, Nick was now able to go through his own alternatives and calculate how much to offer the hospital. He shifted the conversation away from price and focused on addressing all of the hospital's expectations, building a strong case that justified the full value he was offering. The department head liked the way that Nick approached his problem, and the deal eventually closed.

Fast-forward to the next month. The equipment was delivered successfully, it worked perfectly, and the hospital had scheduled training for all of the lab technicians on how to use the new equipment. But here is where Nick almost lost the customer. For a variety of reasons, the technicians kept postponing the training. Nick started to worry. If the technicians couldn't get up to speed quickly, all of the promises Nick had made would start to unravel.

Nick had to shift his thinking. The buying community in the delivering value phase was separated into two groups. The department head had represented the first group. The second group was the team of technicians. They assessed Nick's full value with a completely different set of expectations. Therefore, Nick had to think of alternatives in a different way, defining them from the technicians' perspective, not the department head's.

For the technicians, status quo was almost sacred. They liked the routine. It meant job security and peace of mind. Learning how to run this new equipment meant that they had to work harder, which was not necessarily a key selling point.

But Nick recognized another pattern and became agile. He discovered that, although the technicians were not driven by efficiency, they were keenly driven by quality and accountability. Simply said, they loved their patients. To them, seeing ten extra patients a week was nothing compared to helping another human being receive quality medical care. So Nick blended this aspect into how he promoted the training. It was no longer "come to new medical equipment" training. It was "come to help someone's kid" training. The technicians loved it, and responded accordingly. The impact of the status quo had been successfully replaced with the impact of do-it-yourself, with a nudge from Nick.

Once the training had been completed, the testing schedule improved dramatically. Doctors, patients, and technicians were all happier. And the department head? He asked Nick to come by his office to discuss another possible opportunity.

CONSIDER THIS

Because we're talking about a non-linear pattern-based approach to selling, it's a good idea to revisit alternatives before each and every sales meeting. Alternatives may shift with new information, new individuals within the buyer decision-making process, or market forces (to name a few).

SHIFTING ALTERNATIVES

Can you see how the alternatives kept shifting in Nick's story? More importantly, can you see how Nick used the lens of alternatives to justify his full value? Alternatives kept the conversation moving in a way that was both intentional and intelligent. Nick wasn't trying to close. He was trying to justify his value—all the way through the full value experience.

And you also may have noticed something incredibly important here. Nick kept using expectations and alternatives interdependently. He couldn't work with one without going back to the other.

Being agile is about bringing the lens of expectations and the lens of alternatives together. You must constantly look at everything with both lenses. When you do, you are able to pick a single snowflake out of the chaos and focus on it until you see every minor detail.

But we are not just trying to help you see with greater clarity. These snow goggles have a far greater effect than just better vision, but you'll have to read the next chapter to learn what that is.

Making It Stick

Revisit the same customer you focused on in Chapter 14. Using the lens of alternatives, define your alternatives as they relate to the sales conversations you have had. Then define the buyer's alternatives. Once you define the broad sets of alternatives, think through what other information you need to gather in order to understand the alternatives in greater detail. Write them down.

16

Blending Expectations and Alternatives to Justify Value

"Life can either be accepted or changed. If it is not accepted, it must be changed. If it cannot be changed, then it must be accepted."

Anonymous

INTRODUCTION

As you saw in the last chapter, expectations and alternatives are interdependent and linked together. If you alter one expectation with a person, the alternatives will also be altered. And the same is true for alternatives. Change one alternative (or remove it), and expectations change as well. In fact, we would say that this interdependence is dynamic, making the linkage between expectations and alternatives the most critical element to understand to truly practice the Agility Selling rule of justifying full value. You must be able to intentionally blend expectations and alternatives if you are going to create and defend your value as a master of agility.

TWO WAYS TO BLEND

As a seller, this blending can be accomplished by using one of two methods:

1. Reposition the customer's expectations
2. Reposition the alternatives

Let's look at the first method. This approach works best when what you are trying to sell is being compared to similar offerings. Repositioning the customer's expectations means that you must demonstrate how what you are offering should change their expectations. In other words, show them what they can and cannot have in a way that their expectation actually changes.

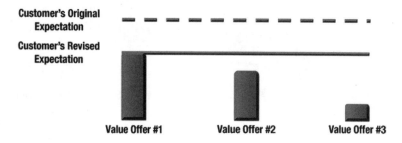

Customer's Original Expectation

Customer's Revised Expectation

Value Offer #1   Value Offer #2   Value Offer #3

Look at the graphic above. Using the airplane ticket example from the last chapter, repositioning the customer's expectation of cost is accomplished by showing how the cost compares to the best value offerings from other airlines (which are all "find someone" alternatives). Notice how Value Offer 1 provides the best possible alternative, even though it is still not as good as what the customer originally expected. This simple side-by-side price comparison repositions the customer's expectation to be far more realistic.

So what happens when the buyer wants to oversimplify cost as just the sticker price? Or what if the prices that a buyer is looking at are all too close to each other? In either case, you can highlight any extra cost charges by the competition (luggage fees when flying, anyone?) or even introduce a different cost lever altogether, such as frequent flier miles with the ability to spend slightly more now and fly free later or perhaps even allow you to reach elite status and be bumped to first-class seating for the original price of flying coach. Now the buyer has a completely different mindset when comparing prices and sees the overall cost with greater clarity. In each of these examples, note how the buyer's simple expectation of cost was repositioned.

The second method, repositioning alternatives, is completely different. Repositioning alternatives means that you will fulfill either more expectations or different expectations so that the customer changes his or her mind about which alternative is best. By increasing the full value of the alternatives you offer, you provide a completely different alternative to the buyer.

Status Quo   **Do-It-Yourself**   **Find Someone**

No Deal   **Sell to Someone Else**   **Close the Deal**

For example, look at the graphic. The initial scenario shows that the buyer's perceived best alternative for an airline ticket is to choose status quo, as the price of the ticket is just too much. But savvy salespeople will expand the conversation with the buyer to include more of his or her expectations. Surely, we reason, cost is not the only consideration, right? Hey, buyer, what about the luxury of the seating (appeal), the safety of the plane (quality), or the perfect schedule that coincides with your vacation dates (efficiency)? The buyer's initial expectations did not change. More were uncovered. If the buyer agrees to include these expectations, the alternatives are now repositioned, as illustrated in the next scenario.

Status Quo   **Do-It-Yourself**   **Find Someone**

No Deal   **Sell to Someone Else**   **Close the Deal**

As we see it, bundling expectations and alternatives to sway the buyer is the crux of justifying your full value. This approach can be used in any selling situation. In fact, this approach can be used during any of the conversations during the sales experience, even with different buyers throughout the buyer's organization. The key is to stay away from focusing on just one expectation at a time and to keep full value at the center of the discussion.

PAY ATTENTION

Bundling of expectations and alternatives to sway the buyer is the crux of justifying your full value.

BUILDING ON THE FOUNDATION

Change is a process, not an event. The concept of behavior change is important when it comes to balancing expectations and alternatives. Sometimes the seller (and the people within the selling organization) will need to change their behavior to respond to the expectations of the buyer. On the other hand, the buyer may change his or her expectations and behavior with the seller. Often overlooked, behavior change is an important concept in professional selling.

Named one of the five most influential authors in psychology by the Institute for Scientific Information and the American Psychological Society, Dr. James Prochaska is one of the originators of the Trans-theoretical Model of Behavior Change (Prochaska & DiClemente, 1983) and the author of more than three hundred papers on behavior change.

Dr. Prochaska determined there are five stages of behavior change. People in the earliest stage are not intending to make a change (pre-contemplation). They may not even be aware that their behavior is unhealthy or they may be demoralized from past failed attempts. People in the final stage have made a change and are working to keep it up (maintenance). And in the middle we have some who are just starting to think about changing their behavior (contemplation), others who have decided to make a behavior change (preparation), and still others who have just begun to take action to change their behavior (action).

Why is this important? Research has shown that up to 80 percent of people are not ready to take action right away. It's something they have to work up to, and not everyone moves at the same pace. People can resist pressure to take action if they are not ready for it.

Source: www.prochange.com/staff/james_prochaska

Bʟᴇɴᴅɪɴɢ Exᴘᴇᴄᴛᴀᴛɪᴏɴs ᴀɴᴅ Aʟᴛᴇʀɴᴀᴛɪᴠᴇs ғᴏʀ Iᴍᴘᴀᴄᴛ

Pause. Can you see what we mean by blending expectations and alternatives? If the full value of the alternative you are offering does not meet expectations better than the other alternatives that exist, value cannot be justified. And if you cannot justify the full value, there probably won't be a deal.

Think of how a car works. The engine provides the power, and the drive shaft transfers the energy to turn the wheels. The engine and the drive shaft have to work together to move the car. In the same way, you need a connection between expectations and alternatives to make the engine of sales work. When your understanding of the customer is limited to his or her expectations, you may have power but no leverage. This is like having a working motor in a car with no drive shaft. The car will just sit while the engine revs. And if your understanding of the customer is limited to his or her alternatives, you may have leverage but no power. This is like having a drive shaft to make the wheels turn, but no motor to actually rotate the drive shaft. The car will sit in silence. You must understand both the expectations and the alternatives to keep the energy going in the sales process. Or, as we like to say, your snow goggles must use both lenses in order to see the patterns clearly.

Here is the tricky bit. Being an agile seller means that you are constantly speaking with buyers in order to gain more understanding of both their expectations and alternatives as they perceive them during the course of the entire buying process.

Just remember, because buyers are human beings, their expectations are probably going to shift over time. For example, the buyer may come across a new product that provides even greater benefits. As a result, the buyer's alternatives will shift as well. A supplier who is able to provide only a specific product line may become obsolete when another supplier can offer the new product in addition to supplying all the customer's original needs.

CONSIDER THIS

Power and leverage are pretty important in a sales relationship. Power provides the momentum to move a conversation forward, while leverage makes the task easier. But note that we are not recommending that you be manipulative. Using power and leverage to manipulate your customers for your own benefit will only weaken your credibility, and we have already talked about what a lack of credibility will do to your long-term viability. Trust us. Sacrificing your credibility for power and leverage will only create more chaos.

This dynamic means that whatever choices a buyer makes during the discover, position, and deliver value phases, there will be a new set of expectations for each phase of the experience—and new alternatives to go with them. What was once a passing topic in an earlier conversation will now be of greater significance for both buyer and seller. You can literally lose (or regain) all of your power and your leverage halfway through a deal.

This brings us to the most complex part of justifying your full value.

To help us explain this concept, we want you to imagine how delivery or implementation requirements can suddenly be vital after a contract is signed. Maybe these requirements were adequately addressed in the contract. Maybe they weren't. But if the customer demands your help in an unexpected way (a shift in expectations), you have to evaluate whether the impact of your alternative is strong enough to respond to the customer demand. Even if you find the demand unreasonable, but your next-best alternative is to lose the deal, you will likely respond. The customer has all the leverage. But what if you can say no and still keep the current business while potentially selling to someone else? You now have the leverage.

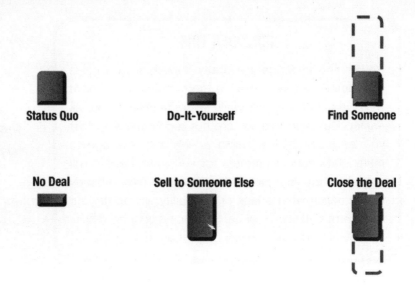

Status Quo   Do-It-Yourself   Find Someone

No Deal   Sell to Someone Else   Close the Deal

If you are a true master of Agility Selling, you will use your leverage to strengthen your relationship with the customer. You will look at the situation and determine whether this crisis can be turned into an opportunity. You will evaluate how to blend the expectations and alternatives to justify your full value in a brand new way that trades what is valuable to the customer (the unexpected help) for what is valuable to you (new business, more customer data, or access to other decision-makers). The bottom line is that you are able to transform the buyer/seller relationship to grow the full value, thereby actually creating new value, not just delivering against the initial transaction.

This is how powerful your understanding of expectations and alternatives can be. The true master of Agility Selling can create the most amazing results, even in the midst of seeming chaos.

PAY ATTENTION

Negotiation doesn't have to be difficult. While it may be challenging, the more you put into understanding the expectations and alternatives you may encounter, the easier negotiations will become.

This is the second rule of Agility Selling. If you understand how to justify your value through the two lenses of expectations and alternatives, you will fundamentally transform the quality of your sales conversations. You will no longer just show up and throw out the same old probing questions. You will no longer be able to dump your offering on the table and hope the customer picks something that sounds good. You will no longer waste your precious time on deals that have better alternatives. You will no longer be able to negotiate the same way. Shucks, you may not have to negotiate price at all in the traditional sense of the tactical back and forth that people waste their hard-earned money trying to be experts at. Ultimately, you will strengthen customer relationships and internal partnerships in powerful ways that transform the entire value experience.

MIRROR MOMENT

Here's your mirror moment. With this new under-standing of expectations and alternatives, how well do you really justify your value? Seriously. Do you intentionally define all six expectations and rigorously seek to understand the six alternatives? If we followed you around, what would we see? Better yet, if we listened to your external and internal conversations, what would we hear? Would those conversations be tightly packaged around identifying, exploring, and defining the expectations and alternatives? Or would we listen to a handful of discussions around expectations here and an alternative there?

To go one step further, how often do you lose either your power or leverage in a deal?

If you are finding either of these elements to be a weakness in how you manage your business, chances are that you do not understand how to blend expectations and alternatives as well as you think you do.

Is your mouth going a little dry? If so, that's ok. Now you see a core problem with how you sell. As we said before, once you identify a problem, it loses half its strength.

Making It Stick

Evaluate the kind of power and leverage you have. Think of an agreement you are working on right now. It can be from any part of the discover, position, and deliver value experience.

How well do you understand all of the buyer's expectations? Are you sure you have uncovered all of them? This evaluation of expectations defines your power for this agreement. If you have a lot of expectations to work with, you have a lot of potential power for this agreement. Conversely, if there are not very many expectations (or the expectations are not very strong), you don't have much to work with here.

Next, how well do you understand the impact of each alternative? Have you taken the time to think through each one of them, even briefly? This evaluation of alternatives defines your leverage for this agreement. Whoever has the best alternative outside of working together has the greater leverage. The ideal scenario is when neither of you has much of an alternative outside of working together. In this case, no one has the advantage. This means that, when you work together, you share your leverage, and the task of finding agreement is actually quite easy.

Finally, what can you do to either generate more power or leverage to possibly create even more value for this agreement? Can you reposition the expectations? Can you reposition the alternatives? If you can, you are on your way to something much greater than what you started with.

CHAPTER

Justifying Value with Agility

"He who controls others may be powerful, but he who has mastered himself is mightier still."

Lao Tzu

INTRODUCTION

In Chapter 12, we took a break in order to wrap up the details of the first rule of Agility Selling that we discussed in Chapters 6 through 12. Now here, in Chapter 17, we'll pause briefly to reflect on the second rule of Agility Selling and what we discussed in Chapters 13 through 16.

REVIEW: AGILITY SELLING

As you remember, in Chapter 12 we provided an overview of how to navigate the first rule of Agility Selling. Remember that Agility Selling is a non-linear, pattern-based approach to selling containing two rules:

1. Instead of focusing on the stages of your sales process, *focus on your selling skills.*

2. Instead of focusing on selling your product or service, *focus on justifying the customer's definition of value.*

Here in Chapter 17, we recap the second rule.

Justify Full Value

In Chapter 13 we picked up our conversation of full value, the entire bundle of expectations that drive the buyer through discovering, positioning, and delivering value. This concept is important because it redefines the boundaries of the buying/selling relationship. Instead of trying to solve problems related to the transaction, sellers can be seen as solving problems related to the full value experience.

Let's face it. Full value is important. Your customers want more than the solution you are selling. They want the entire experience, and they will complain when they don't get it (remember the Starbucks Effect we discussed in Chapter 13?).

It's not *your* expectations that define value. It's the *buyer's* expectations that define value as he or she attempts to solve a problem. Whenever a customer complains about something, it is almost always tied to his or her expectations of full value.

PAY ATTENTION

The six expectations that determine how customers define full value are:

- Satisfaction
- Cost
- Appeal
- Quality
- Efficiency
- Accountability

Six Buyer Expectations

In Chapter 14, we covered the six buyer expectations and discussed how to manage them. We agreed that, long before you present a solution and long after you close the deal, all buyers have expectations, right? The six buyer expectations are constantly shifting throughout the customer's relationship with you, and they are rooted in the fact that he or she expects a lot when buying your product or service. The relationship the buyer will have with you is much bigger than benefits promised or a calculation of the total cost of ownership. You don't just sell a product or service; you actually sell an experience.

The six expectations that determine how customers define full value are:

- Satisfaction
- Cost
- Appeal
- Quality
- Efficiency
- Accountability

Six Alternatives

In Chapter 15, we looked at the six alternatives and how to leverage them. We discussed how the six alternatives are broken into two groups.

The first group of alternatives is focused on the buyer. Generally speaking, every buyer has three alternatives:

- Remain with the "status quo"
- Choose to "do-it-yourself"
- Decide to "find someone" to help

The next set of three alternatives is focused on you, the seller. Generally speaking, every seller has three alternatives to any given opportunity:

- Reach "no agreement"
- Choose to sell to "someone else"
- "Close" the opportunity

To leverage alternatives, start by identifying the impacts of both sides' alternatives. Assume that a deal will be made. This means that the alternatives of "find someone" and "close" line up. Evaluating the impact of the buyer's other alternatives (which include finding someone other than you) will quickly show you how desirable your offer is to the buyer. But don't stop there. Evaluate the impact of your own alternatives. This will help you see how much you should be willing to offer to the buyer.

After you have a sense of what to offer, keep using the lens of alternatives to track the deal as it develops. The last thing you want is an alternative to pop up out of nowhere.

CONSIDER THIS

The idea of expectations and alternatives applies throughout the full value experience. Do not limit your efforts to simply reaching the point at which your customer agrees to buy from you. An agile seller proactively addresses each of these expectations and alternatives before it leads to a customer complaint.

Blending Expectations and Alternatives

In Chapter 16, we talked about how to blend expectations and alternatives to create and defend your value. As a seller, this can be accomplished using one of two methods:

1. Reposition the customer's expectations
2. Reposition the alternatives

Repositioning the customer's expectations works best when you are being compared to similar alternatives (like find someone). Repositioning the customer's expectations works best when all of the alternatives are still under discussion.

If the total alternatives being discussed do not meet expectations better than the alternatives that exist off the table, value cannot be justified. If you cannot justify the full value, there will be no deal. This concept applies to both buyer and seller.

Just remember that expectations constantly shift. As a consequence, so do alternatives. With whatever choices a buyer makes, there will be a new set of expectations for each phase of the value experience—and new alternatives to go with them. What was once a passing topic in an earlier conversation will now be of greatest significance for both sides of the deal.

When you are able to effectively blend alternatives and expectations, you can begin to create value where none previously existed. You will find yourself transforming the conversations that you have with your customers. You will be able to influence these conversations, allowing you to see where power and leverage exist. This will help you determine next steps to create the best exchange of value. This is what it means to be an "agile seller."

BUILDING ON THE FOUNDATION

We have found that, when expectations and alternatives are balanced, quality improves. Quality is an important concept for both the buyer and the seller.

At a time when fellow quality gurus Deming, Juran, and Ishikawa were focused on the highly technical aspects of quality measurement and control, Philip Crosby's book *Quality Is Free* (Crosby, 1979) hit the bookstores with a simple but powerful message:

- Quality is much too important to be left to the quality control department;
- Senior management must commit to quality if things are to change; and
- Doing things right the first time adds absolutely nothing to the cost of a product or service.

Crosby showed managers everywhere that doing things wrong made costs skyrocket. More importantly, he showed that management was the root cause of these problems.

The book set off a revolution in corporate thinking because it shifted the responsibility for the quality of goods and services from the quality control department to the corporate boardroom, attacked the entrenched notions of "good enough" and "acceptable quality levels" (AQL), and introduced "zero defects" as the only acceptable performance standard, setting the stage for the Six Sigma movement that followed.

Source: www.philipcrosby.com/pca/C.Press.html

Making It Stick

Creating a Journal Entry

Take a moment to reflect on what we have been discussing. We have used a lot of stories and examples and discussed habits and principles you need to be successful. Before moving on to the next chapter, take a moment and reflect.

Using the space provided, write some notes to yourself:

1. What are your key takeaways from Chapters 13 through 16?

2. Have you identified any areas that you personally want to improve? What are they?

3. Do you know someone who can discuss this with you?

4. In the next ninety days, what are your top two or three priorities?

SECTION
4

Agility Selling in Action

Agile Sales Conversations

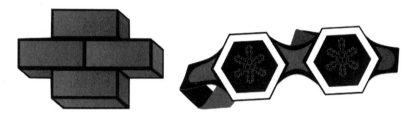

*"Conversation is an art in which a man has all mankind
for competitors."*

Ralph Waldo Emerson

INTRODUCTION

So let's put it all together. We've given you the ability to think differently using elements of chaos theory with butterflies, anchor points, and snowflakes. Knowing–and recognizing–these patterns will help you slow the chaos down. And we have given you two very powerful rules for selling differently:

1. Instead of focusing on the stages of your sales process, *focus on your selling skills.*

2. Instead of focusing on selling your product or service, *focus on justifying the customer's definition of value.*

Now we want to take these concepts to the next level and talk about how to apply them in agile conversations.

Ready? Here we go.

CHANGING YOUR BEHAVIOR

As we have already said, sales conversations can occur at any time with any buyer during the conversations required to justify full value. Just as a reminder, we call this *the full value experience*.

We know how hard it can be to change your behavior. It's such a hard concept that Brian actually researches this subject full-time while helping sales teams all over the world change the way they sell. It's easier said than done.

So what if we simplified the concept of agile conversation in a way that enables you to change your behavior more easily. What if we gave you a tool to drive all of your sales conversations toward the topics that create the most agility? This tool would help you actually see through the clutter of the average working day and determine which conversations give you the greatest chance of sales success. Oh, and what if this tool will help you turn these agile conversations into more accurate sales forecasts?

Yeah, we figured that would get your attention.

CONSIDER THIS

An effective sales conversation allows buyers to receive the information they need at the time they need it and contains two parts. First, the conversation allows you to engage the buyers in an open discussion about issues that are most important to them. Second, the sales conversation allows you to listen to what is most important and most real to the buyer.

Let's unpack the idea of sales conversations with different people.

Pause. Notice that we didn't use the word "customers." We did that on purpose. If you are going to be truly agile, you are going to have to let the forces of the non-linear, full value, and community expand your concept of professional selling just a wee bit more.

FOCUSING ON THE SALES CONVERSATION

Here's a simple exercise for you. Picture a sales conversation. Can you see it? Who is there? How many people? What is being talked about? Seriously, pause and picture this conversation as if it were happening in front of you right now.

Got it? Ok. Read on.

If you are like most salespeople, when we ask you to think of a sales conversation, you picture yourself talking directly with a customer. In fact, you'll do this even if the customer is just a prospect who hasn't officially bought anything yet. It's our guess that, if you took this little exercise seriously, you struggled a bit with deciding what the conversation was about. Why? Because you have an entire snowflake to play around in. But perhaps you didn't think the conversation entailed *discovering value* or *delivering value*. If that's the case, your default view of a sales conversation is probably locked into just *positioning value.* That basically means you're a walking, talking brochure. And maybe (oh, this hurts to say) some of you reading this automatically pictured a sales pitch. You know what a sales pitch is, right? It's a salesperson (or team of salespeople) verbally dumping a canned, pre-packaged load of features and facts on a buyer (or even buying team) in sixty minutes or less. PowerPoint deck not necessarily included.

The sad truth is that it is far too common for people, both sellers and buyers, to reduce the concept of a sales conversation to the term "sales pitch." That is not a sales conversation. But neither are the conversations you can have with a customer that basically set you up to deliver a sales pitch.

Think about it. We should all agree by now that customers are really not interested in being sold. In today's economy, we would say that your most important customers aren't really interested in buying either. Money is far too precious these days. So the first part of defining a sales conversation is the topic, which is *not* your product or service.

If you are being agile, you have been using your Four Habits of Agile Sellers to set up a sales conversation. The topic of that sales conversation is the stuff that creates full value: expectations and alternatives, as in understanding what expectations and alternatives exist in discovering value, positioning value, and delivering value. A sales conversation is focused on everything that will help you blend expectations and alternatives to justify full value. If you limit the conversation to your products or services, you are actually limiting your value.

But if you limit the concept of a sales conversation to just a buyer and seller discussing how to position full value, you are still short of what we are getting at. You have to expand your definition of sales conversations to include anyone who can help you blend expectations and alternatives to justify full value. We typically call these people buyers because they can influence the buying decision. Oh, and guess what, with all the buyers you need to talk with on the buyer side, you also need to identify internal resources within your own company and align these resources with the buyers.

PAY ATTENTION

For you to be effective, you'll have to have valuable sales conversations externally with your buyers, and you'll have to have valuable conversations internally as well.

AGILE SALES CONVERSATIONS

Think for a moment of all of the people who can help you reposition either expectations or alternatives. Just looking at your own organization, you will see a long list of teammates, including other salespeople, your manager, finance, legal, IT, customer service, distribution, and others. And as we have already pointed out, buyers have their own sets of teammates. When it comes to the most profitable deals, the biggest deal-breaker isn't whether or not you were able to get the buyer and seller talking. It's having the *right* sales conversations, and aligning the *right* resources within the full value experience. That means you must manage the right internal and external people, even if the most important decision-maker isn't in the room.

So there are two parts of the sales conversation. One part is external, focused on the buyer, and the other part is internal, focused on your own internal resources. If you aren't talking about the right things with both buyers and internal resources, your conversation isn't going to produce anything. And you should be talking about more than the topic of buying. You should be talking about the two most critical aspects of justifying full value—expectations and alternatives.

Once the right people have agreed on how to justify full value, the entire sales relationship can move forward—and generate revenue, which is the purpose of this whole drill, remember?

CONSIDER THIS

While the sales process moves through distinct phases, the conversations within those phases require you to be in tune with the buyer. Although many salespeople focus on qualifying leads, making presentations, negotiating, closing, and following up, Agile Sellers focus on the quality and relevance of the sales conversation, staying focused on the buyer's problem-solving process.

Can you see how using your four core habits with anyone involved in repositioning expectations or alternatives for the purpose of justifying full value will create agility? You are responding to the moment with the best possible approach. You also have the extra bonus of slowing the chaos down enough to see patterns emerge, patterns that will show you how to accelerate sales success and avoid tornadoes.

We know, you want the checklist. We didn't forget.

PAY ATTENTION

Great questions help you request information from the buyer. That information will ultimately help you balance alternatives and expectations in justifying value.

Here it is. We call this checklist "The Fifteen Questions," for obvious reasons, five questions for each crystal of the snowflake. You can use them in a linear, process-driven way if you want to. Just don't forget to allow the chaos to randomly shift on you. And here is the good news. You can also use the fifteen questions in a non-linear and pattern-based way that allows you to be agile in the chaos.

One final caution. We will give these questions to you if you agree to revisit your sales activities based on the answers to these questions. For example, if you don't know the answers, you shouldn't be forecasting anything to close. More often than not, by the time we are through asking folks the first few questions, their forecast for the next ninety days is already falling apart. We have walked people through random account activity and found that the deals that were supposedly locked in were experiencing unexpected delays. Something was missing — like the answers to these questions. If that's the case, it's ok. Just refocus.

DISCOVER VALUE QUESTIONS

Ok. Let's started with the first five questions. These questions are linked to the Discover Value phase. Remember that by the end of this phase, the customer will agree on what value is needed. You will exercise your Four Habits of Agile Sellers to determine the expectations buyers have and the alternatives that exist in relation to seeking value. Remember that you are not trying to actively sell anything here. You are simply trying to justify the full value.

The discover value questions are:

1. What problem(s) are we addressing, and how high of a priority are they?

2. Who are they important to, what are their expectations, and how will they measure success?

3. What are the impacts of the alternatives, and what is our plan to address them?

4. What value must be communicated to compel the buyer to buy from us?

5. What buying steps must the customer go through to turn this opportunity into revenue, and how are you managing each step?

Notice that the questions use your four habits to create a sense of the classic who, what, when, etc. The picture that is generated by answering these questions will not only help you justify full value, but also determine whether or not you even want this deal. This perspective is vital, but we will discuss more about that in a moment.

Let's look at the first question: What problem(s) are we addressing, and how high is their priority? Identifying the problems is a basic selling concept, but the sense of priority is not. How often have you seen a salesperson become excited about a potential sales opportunity that he is absolutely convinced exists, yet find himself eventually sputtering out a month or two later because, when he made his pitch, the customer shrugged and walked away? The opportunity was real, but it wasn't a priority. So don't just find the problems. Once you identify the problems, continue probing until you know what level of priority the buyer is giving to each of them.

Second question: Who are they important to, what are their expectations, and how will they measure success? Obviously, you want to know who the decision-makers and influencers are and, by now, you should also want to know how they view all six expectations. But do you take it a step further and look at how they will measure success? Notice we are not saying that the buyers' own measurements will be effective. In fact, this may be a point for you to reposition their expectations by focusing on what is measured. For example, some buyers only look at making a purchase that meets budget requirements (cost), but you can introduce the added benefit of strategic business impact (like quality, efficiency, and accountability). Remember, you are trying to get the customer to agree on what value is needed, not just the value stated in the request for proposal (RFP). This also means that you will be looking at the buyer's overall business. You must understand how it works and how the full value you offer fits in. If you miss this insight, you might become stuck with just one expectation, and that is a lousy position to be in.

Third question: What are the impacts of the alternatives, and what is our plan to address them? Once again, there are six alternatives, and you want to know what the best ones are for you and for the buyer. With the "why" and "who" sorted out from answers to the first two questions, you should have enough information to figure out the impact of the status quo, do-it-yourself, and find someone alternatives. You can also begin to determine the impacts of your alternatives: no deal, someone else, and close. And close does not mean sign an agreement at this point. You are in the discover value phase, so the close alternative just means being considered for providing the full value the buyer needs.

By understanding the answers to these questions, you can determine both where the leverage currently sits and what you need to do to justify your full value. For example, let's say you decide that your only legitimate alternative is to close, but an analysis of your customer's alternatives shows that the impact of maintaining the status quo is almost as strong as the impact of finding someone. In this situation you will need to reposition expectations and alternatives to minimize the value of status quo and make the value the customer will agree to.

Fourth question: What value must be communicated to compel the buyer to buy from us? Picking up from the place that the answers to the third question led us, we now switch from a big picture analysis to a detailed plan of action. The full value we are looking to define will need input from a number of folks on your own sales team, not just the buyers. And don't limit the value to just what is important now. Think of what expectations and alternatives will come into focus as the value experience develops. Don't overemphasize these bits, but don't ignore them either. Build a package that creates a sense of intrigue that the buyer will want to know more about.

Fifth question: What buying steps must the customer go through to turn this opportunity into revenue, and how are you managing each step? Finally, a linear question. Well, not really, because we know that buyers rarely go through a linear process when making decisions. When they have a problem to solve, they'll approach buying with a much broader view than most salespeople will, that's for sure. So if you map out the buying steps as touch points, rather than as a process, you should be able to decide how to manage these steps if they occur in either a linear or a non-linear way. More importantly, you should have a sense of where the potential obstacles may be so that you can plan to address them in advance. Unless you like to wait for butterflies to turn into tornadoes. But we digress.

If you can answer at least four of these questions, you will be in a good position to create momentum for this opportunity. If you only know the answers to two (or fewer) questions, you are in a dark place—a very dark place indeed. If you actually persuade the customer to acknowledge and agree on their legitimate needs, consider yourself lucky, not skilled.

For those of you thinking about having only three questions answered, flip a coin. Your odds of success are that random.

It is important to have a sense of how high a priority this deal is in comparison to the other deals you are working on. Face it, you only have so much time in a day. The last thing you need is a bad deal creating unnecessary chaos in your day. If the only value you discover from this opportunity is limited or will take too long to develop, don't waste your time on it today. Move on to something else until the value grows or becomes achievable.

POSITION VALUE QUESTIONS

Now, let's go to the position value phase because there is a genuine possibility that you may have the chance to build from your work in discover value. Even if the sales conversation begins here, you can still operate with agility. Remember, by the end of this phase, the customer will define what the best deal looks like. This means that you will be exercising all of your four habits to blend expectations and alternatives in a way that maximizes the value you are trying to justify.

BUILDING ON THE FOUNDATION

BUILDING ON THE FOUNDATION

Neil Rackham first gained international recognition when he led the largest-ever research study of successful selling and sales effectiveness in the 1970s. This massive project, supported by major multinationals including Xerox and IBM, involved a team of thirty researchers who studied 35,000 sales calls in more than twenty countries. The research took twelve years at a cost, in today's dollars, of $30 million. From the results of these studies, Rackham published the groundbreaking classics *SPIN Selling* (1988) and *Major Account Sales Strategy* (1989). His books regularly rank among business bestsellers. He is also author of more than fifty influential articles on marketing, selling, and channel strategy.

The SPIN® Model for developing needs includes:

- Situation questions
- Problem questions
- Implication questions
- Need-payoff questions.

Source: www.huthwaite.com

The position value questions are:

6. What is the best possible exchange of value for both sides?
7. What value are we willing to trade or reposition to achieve agreement?
8. What realistic options can we present to keep the exchange of value in alignment with our desired business results?
9. How do these options impact the buyer's desired business results?
10. What negotiation issues do we expect them to raise, and what is our plan for dealing with those?

Notice how the answers to these questions help you build an informed, deliberate plan that relies heavily on your four habits. These questions also provide answers that will fit into any formal sales process that you may still be using. In fact, it should make your sales process more robust, for those of you who care.

Sixth question: What is the best possible exchange of value for both sides? In other words, if you could give your customer the biggest, best, most creative definition of full value in exchange for the biggest, best, most creative bundle of what the customer can offer you, what expectations would be included?

This question gets to the heart of full value. Being able to accurately answer it means that you have used your four habits to uncover all of the expectations a customer can have and can now put together the kind of proposal that really separates you from the competition. But it also brings your own perspective in. By determining how much value the buyer can legitimately achieve, and how much value you can legitimately offer, you should have a fairly decent sense of what you are willing to trade for.

Seventh question: What value are we willing to trade or reposition to achieve agreement? Once you have a sense of everything that can be on the negotiating table, define the priorities and limitations. By determining which customer expectations are non-negotiable and which are fair game, you should be able to decide what you are willing to use in setting up a deal.

For example, consider the customer who wants five big expectations met (one satisfaction element, two cost elements, an efficiency element, and an accountability element). After analyzing the alternatives, you realize that the customer can really only address four of those expectations (the efficiency element in this scenario is something that no one can provide). An examination of your alternatives reveals that you want at least three things from the customer (money, contracted purchasing levels, and access to customer data) in exchange for meeting the four expectations. Thinking about expectations and alternatives in this kind of detail will help you reposition them to give you maximum power and leverage before any negotiations begin–unless you like to wait until the Starbuck's Effect takes over and the customer demands to have everything for one low price.

Eighth question: What realistic options can we present to keep the exchange of value in alignment with our desired business results? This is your gut check. You used the previous questions to figure out what a perfect world would look like. Now you have to be more practical. Offering to meet a customer expectation that your own organization does not want to fulfill is only going to turn into a broken promise. Take the time to figure out which obstacles can be removed and which will have to be left alone. It is very possible that you will have to go back to the seventh question and recalibrate your answer. Don't fight this. Embrace it. You are being agile, remember?

This also means that you are starting to create multiple offers based on your customer's definition of full value. For example, you may offer to address only some of the expectations if cost is the biggest driver. You might want to create an offer that allows you to address other expectations and ignore cost altogether. Finally, you may also want to create an offer that not only addresses the customer's definition of full value, but also pushes her toward a more innovative, outside-the-box solution. Presenting realistic multiple offers allows you to test the validity of your own conclusions while you attempt to maximize the value. There's nothing wrong with allowing the customer to define what the best deal looks like. In fact, it's encouraged.

Ninth question: How do these options impact the buyer's desired business results? Test your assumptions about the perceived value of the options you are presenting by examining their impact on the buyer's business. Don't be overly optimistic. In fact, we like to look at both best case and worst case answers.

Don't stop at defining the initial impacts. Walk through the consequences of each impact. Create a chain of events that will help you identify potential shifts in the buyer's expectations in the future. This line of thinking will naturally lead back to the team of people you are working with who will support the potential customer. Obtain their input as early as you can. Pick their brains on the impacts they see and how they would address or manage them. They may help you come up with something creative to add to the deal or possibly advise you to pull away to avoid unnecessary risks.

Tenth question: What negotiation issues do we expect them to raise, and what is our plan for dealing with those? We wish we could tell you that customers will stay focused on the full value you are trying to justify, but someone will inevitably try to play some sort of mind game with you during negotiation and ask you to focus on a single expectation. How many mind games are out there? Too many to count. Instead of trying to create a plan for each one, simply work with your team to identify which expectations will be likely to come up and how you think the customer will try to bring them up. If it helps, think about what the customer has done in the past. Make sure that everyone is ready to see the tactic for what it is; then prepare your plan to turn the conversation back to the full value you are trying to justify. When you hear the buyer using a tactic, use some of the following phrases to refocus the discussion on the bigger bundle of expectations:

- "There might be a way to address that if...."
- "We can address that point, and we would also like...."
- "How can we start to...."
- "Please tell me why/when we can get that information...."

The key is to prepare to keep the conversation moving in a way that doesn't disregard the customer demand. Instead, it pulls the demand back into the greater bundle of value you are working with.

The original rules apply to forecasting with these five questions. Four or five quality answers mean that you are prepared to move the deal forward because the customer has defined what the best deal looks like. Anything less than four solid answers means that you are not in a very strong position. We even recommend that you not formally present anything to the customer at this point because you may do more harm than good. You have an incredibly high chance of either stumbling into closing a bad deal or, worse, being used. And by "used" we mean having a customer who will immediately take your proposal and use it to secure a better deal from a current supplier.

DELIVER VALUE QUESTIONS

Let's continue our discussion with the deliver value questions. If you recall, the main purpose of this phase is to get the customer to agree on the impact of the value you provided. This means that you are still using your four habits and the twin lenses of expectations and alternatives to leverage your success in a way that creates more business. Even if customers do not ask you to be involved in this aspect of the full value experience, they are still going to go through it, so use these questions to help you be agile while the value you promised is turned into reality.

The deliver value questions are:

11. What relevant value do we want credit for?

12. What are the important issues to the customer today? Who are they important to, and why?

13. What alternatives does the customer have to address the issues?

14. What new opportunities do the changing issues present to us?

15. How are we following up on these opportunities?

Notice how the answers to these questions give you the chance to not only stay on top of the customer's experience, but also to focus on shifts in either expectations or alternatives. Furthermore, you can use these questions in any number of back office or customer meetings in a way that isn't just about checking in on potential issues with implementation. You can turn these conversations into a whole new discover value experience. Wouldn't that be nice?

Let's review the questions in greater detail.

Eleventh question: What relevant value do we want credit for? You promised results. This is where you measure them. Specifically, look at both quantitative and qualitative measures. *Quantitative* measures are the ones that can be written as hard, objective numbers. *Qualitative* measures can only be defined in soft, subjective terms. Both measures are important. Just make sure that the customer agrees on their validity and is willing to give you credit for a job well done (if it is deserved). You don't want to ignore measuring your impact because it will erode your credibility. Empty promises are not converted into new business.

Twelfth question: What are the important issues to the customer today? Who are they important to, and why? Again, be prepared for shifts. What was important before may no longer be discussed, and what was ignored before may now be a part of every conversation. Don't just identify the shifts; get inside them. Figure out who is driving them and why they are important. This doesn't always mean that senior leadership is involved, but you may discover the need to involve them. The key is that you are being proactive before any butterflies turn into tornadoes.

Thirteenth question: What alternatives does the customer have to address the issues? Whether the issue is a butterfly or an opportunity, you must assess how you should be involved. If the customer decides to find someone, you should be prepared to step in, especially if the full value you are trying to justify is about to fall to pieces. You may even have to analyze the alternatives for each expectation individually to get a stronger sense of where to put your energy first. When we say analyze, we mean figure out the impacts. Knowing these will help you accurately address the next question.

Fourteenth question: What new opportunities do the changing issues present to us? Not every shift is a crisis. In fact, you can often create unplanned value during the deliver value phase—if you are looking for it. This value may be part of your original deal or it may be something that will spark a whole new discover value discussion. Either way, if the value is justified, start looking for places to put your resources, including the people on your team.

Fifteenth question: How are we following up on these opportunities? Do we really need to expand on this? Probably not, but we do want to emphasize ways that you can manage the follow-up. First, decide what the follow-up is going to be. Generally speaking, it will be one of three choices: *continue* what you are doing, *stop* what you are doing, or *change* what you are doing. Continuing means that you are reinforcing the use of resources in a way that keeps the opportunity thriving, for example, keep the people on the support team working with the customer. Stopping means that you are removing resources in a way that keeps the opportunity from dying, for example, stop trying to over-manage the situation with unnecessary processes. Changing means that you are adjusting the use of resources in a way that grows the opportunity, for example, reassign a team member or improve a process in order to create greater positive impact.

Once you figure out the most appropriate follow-up, track it. Measure it. And if at all possible, learn from it. If you create a best practice, you should add it to your toolkit for the next time you deliver value. Although you may not necessarily use it to create unplanned value now, you will likely be able to create unplanned value with another opportunity in the future.

Now the likelihood that you will use this information to forecast is almost zero. Forecasts typically stop tracking opportunities once they go to contract. But if you are a committed sales professional, you will use this information to assess how good a job you are doing. And the same rule we used earlier applies here: Anything less than four solid answers indicates risk and possible poor performance.

That's it. Fifteen questions to test whether you are truly being an Agile Seller. Every topic we covered is critical to the success of the full value experience. And the answers to these questions are far more important to both you and your customers than the typical data points used in sales. By answering these questions, you are both addressing and forecasting customer needs. This will help you determine which conversations should be happening now and which conversations you should be scheduling for the future. In other words, these fifteen conversations help you to be agile.

Very important to the idea of agile conversations is the concept of *relevance*. Traditionally, folks want to benchmark and forecast their business performance with historical data. The emphasis is put on past and current trends (like closing rates, length of sales cycle, and performance against prior years). While this approach is very pragmatic, we have found that customers care far more about relevance than they do about contributing to your trending data. Furthermore, calculating trends can lull you into treating bigger, complex deals as average. And bigger, complex deals are usually anything but average.

We are not talking about throwing historical data out the door. We are simply not going to obsess about it (or use it as the definitive benchmark for today's reality). Instead, we suggest you use *relevance* as the centerpiece of your agility, that is, the things that have the most significance both to your customer and to your own business. We hope that by now you see the Four Habits of Agile Sellers and justifying value generating agile conversations as the most significant thing for both parties.

To put it another way, your customers want you to master influence, insight, execution, and credibility if you are going to be the kind of salesperson they want to work with. And so will your employer. Your using the four habits to blend expectations and alternatives in a way that creates and defends full value will have a far greater impact on your performance than any other sales activity. In fact, without these principles in action, all other sales activity will lack relevance. To put it in more traditional terms, your closing rate will shrink, your length of sales cycle will gradually increase, and your performance against prior years will have more to do with the economy than with your actual skill. That's not the kind of seller we want you to be. But if you can get these bits right, the conversations you are part of will genuinely drive your success.

Agile conversations. Don't go to work without them.

Making It Stick

When it comes to agile sale conversations, the fifteen questions help you plan effectively so you can better understand the customer's problem as well as the customer's problem solving and buying processes. The answers to the questions below provide a planning tool to help you with your sales process.

Discover Value Questions

1. What problem(s) are we addressing, and how high of a priority are they?

2. Who are they important to, what are their expectations, and how will they measure success?

3. What are the impacts of the alternatives, and what is our plan to address them?

4. What value must be communicated to compel the buyer to buy from us?

5. What buying steps must the customer go through to turn this opportunity into revenue, and how are you managing each step?

Position Value Questions

6. What is the best possible exchange of value for both sides?

7. What value are we willing to trade or reposition to achieve agreement?

8. What realistic options can we present to keep the exchange of value in alignment with our desired business results?

9. How do these options impact the buyer's desired business results?

10. What negotiation issues do we expect them to raise, and what is our plan for dealing with those?

Deliver Value Questions

11. What relevant value do we want credit for?

12. What are the important issues to the customer today? Who are they important to, and why?

13. What alternatives does the customer have to address the issues?

14. What new opportunities do the changing issues present to us?

15. How are we following up on these opportunities?

19

Conclusion

INTRODUCTION

So how have we done? We began this book with a premise that the level of random complexity in the world of business had reached a point at which the three forces of chaos (the non-linear, full value, and community) were out of control. Frankly, they were never really in control to begin with, but at least the demands placed on you as a sales professional meant that you could pretend that you were on top of things with some level of regularity.

That perspective is no longer helpful to produce the kind of successes you may once have produced. Old school strategies and tactics are just that – old. But in this swirling mass of chaos, something new has emerged.

A SINGLE THOUGHT

It began with a single thought. What if chaos is good? What if random complexity is not the enemy, but a competitive asset instead? Could it be possible to thrive in the chaos, to actually harness it?

This requires a radical new way of thinking. We hope that, as you read about Sales Chaos Theory, your mind started to open to the possibilities that chaos provides you. Perhaps the best thing about chaos is that it isn't just a tangled mess. It has patterns that appear over and over again, even if not in a predictable way. Once you know these patterns, you can use them to thrive in the chaos.

The first pattern we talked about was how butterflies create tornadoes. Even the tiniest fluctuations in your people, time, energy, and resources (PTER) can create major disruptions later. But as we said repeatedly, once you understand a problem it loses half of its strength. This means that if you keep your eyes on the PTER in your most important customer relationships, you can see tornadoes before they develop. You may even have the opportunity to address these elements to keep them from becoming tornadoes. You can start eliminating some of the tornadoes in your business. You can slow the chaos down.

The second pattern we talked about was how chaos always has pockets of pattern density, which we called anchor points. The chaos may swirl in unpredictable ways, but it will always stay close to your anchor points. This means that no matter how chaotic your business may be at any given moment, you can find safety by tying into your fundamentals, processes, relationships, and technology—as long as you do it in that order.

Think about it. As soon as you recognize that your business is about to be hammered by the chaos (or is already starting to drift), you have the best way to create stability already in your back pocket. Even if you can only secure two anchors, you can stop spinning wildly. As you secure all of your anchors, you can, and will, use this pattern to create a platform for your agility—a platform that your competitors are likely missing.

Finally, we talked about the third pattern, symbolized by the snowflake. Admit it. Snowflakes are an easier way to remember the idea of fractal mathematics, right? The idea is that you can get infinite possibilities in a finite space. This pattern defines the basic customer experience while recognizing that your most important customer experiences are anything but basic.

No matter how each customer experience develops, they will all have three parts: discovering, positioning, and delivering value.

And while your most transactional, uncomplicated customers will likely build their snowflakes in an old-fashioned, linear way, your most complex, most profitable customers will build their snowflakes randomly. This means that you can either try to force customers to do what you want (which will only irritate them) or you can be rigidly flexible—rigid enough to be trustworthy and flexible enough to be useful.

This means that you can trust the snowflake pattern. Allowing the customer to shift the conversation away from what you expected does not translate into being lazy or indecisive. It means that you are giving the customer what he or she needs most at that specific moment. Once the customer experiences the value he or she is looking for, you will be able to go back to where you left off and complete the snowflake. In fact, the customer will want you to.

Can you see how these three patterns require you to think differently? We guess that they weren't taught to you as part of your new employee orientation. In fact, you were probably taught things that are the polar opposites of these dynamics, so it isn't too much of a stretch to think that you have been trying to live by these polar opposites. How's that working for you?

PATTERNS ARE YOUR FRIEND

Let's face it. If you are really going to use these patterns to help you make sense of the chaos, you will have to find where your thinking has to change. Chances are that, if your thinking is limited, it will be because you are disregarding one (or more) of the three forces of chaos. If you are struggling with recognizing butterflies, anchor points, or snowflakes as they appear all around you, it is probably because you want things to be linear, you want to be responsible for selling the items on your price list, or you want to deal with only one person in the buying-selling relationship.

But if you can embrace all three forces, you can see the patterns with ease. And once you *see* the patterns, you can *understand* the patterns. When you reach this point, you are ready to follow the two rules of Agility Selling and begin to sell differently.

AGILITY SELLING RULES REVISITED

Rule 1

The first rule of Agility Selling is "Instead of focusing on the stages of your sales process, focus on your selling skills." When we say "selling skills," we mean your four habits. Use your habit of *influence* to move sales conversations forward and do stuff through others. Learn how conformity can set your influence in motion and bring motivation into the equation. Use your habit of *insight* to see beyond the obvious to ask better questions and make better decisions. Actively remove assumption and intentionally expand your perspective until you have the clarity you need. Use your habit of *execution* to deliver the full value experience you planned to give your customers. Know where you are going, where you are, and how to keep yourself on track (even when you experience detours). Finally, use your habit of *credibility* to prove your effectiveness and keep your other habits alive. Let your credibility enlarge the impact of your other habits.

Just remember to do it all with balance—both kinds. The first type of balance refers to being neither too weak nor too strong in your use of a habit. The second type of balance refers to the need to keep all four habits running side-by-side. Don't be a one-trick pony.

If you understand the patterns well, your four habits have even more impact. Use your habit of influence to become a butterfly that creates positive changes, to gather support for your anchor points, or even to keep a snowflake growing. Use your habit of insight to discover where the butterflies are coming from, where the anchors may be coming loose, or how the snowflake is shaped. Use your habit of execution to manage the butterflies as they appear, reset your anchor points, or deliver the snowflake you promised. And use your habit of credibility to minimize the number of butterflies that appear, set your very first anchor point, and create new snowflakes.

In other words, the chaos patterns will help to use your habits to obtain the biggest impact. We can promise you that, if you bring all of these habits into the chaos with you, the increase in your performance will be immediate. You will see results in ways that will surprise you. But don't stop there. You still have a chance to maximize the value you are working with, not just to increase it.

Rule 2

Which brings us to the second rule of Agility Selling: "Instead of focusing on selling your product or service, focus on justifying the customer's definition of full value." Because the snowflake represents the full value experience, we gave you a pair of snow goggles to help you see individual snowflakes you are working with. The snow goggles have two lenses: the lens of expectations and the lens of alternatives. Yes, you must know the six expectations and the six alternatives, but more importantly, you must know how to blend them together to meet the customer's definition of value.

This task of justifying value can be accomplished in one of two ways. You can either reposition the customer's expectations or reposition the alternatives. Each method has its own set of requirements, but with practice, you will become more and more agile in how you justify value. In fact, you will soon find yourself not only defending the value you provide, but creating whole new experiences with it. Your customers will treat you differently than they treat their other suppliers, even to the point at which they will use the term "partner" without either of you wincing.

Finally, if you have fully embraced the idea of thinking and selling differently, you will be ready to engage in fifteen powerful conversations, all of which help you turn theory into revenue. The fifteen questions that lead to these conversations not only redefine what you should be talking with your customers about, but they redefine what you should be talking about with your own internal team. If you can find the answers to these fifteen questions, how you sell will fundamentally change. How you forecast will fundamentally change. All because of a tiny, little idea called *relevance*.

THINKING AND SELLING DIFFERENTLY—NOW WHAT?

Here is where we potentially have a major problem. Thinking and selling differently is going to get you in trouble. Try showing up at work and start talking about chaos patterns. Start challenging your own status quo with the concept of relevance. You are going to receive some weird looks. Or worse. Your manager may tell you that you are being foolish. You may be told to clear your mind of all this chaos rubbish – and finish that sales funnel while you're at it.

You see, Agility Selling involves change. It's not that people don't like change. Shucks, people change all the time, as long as it is on their own terms. What people don't like is *being changed*.

You are going to have to make some choices. First, you will have to decide what kind of outcomes you really want. Do you want the pat on the back from working harder and longer to encounter unpredictable slivers of achievement or do you want to take a chance on experiencing the full-blown success we have continuously seen (and experienced ourselves) when folks tap into the chaos? If you choose the latter, be prepared for initial isolation. In fact, we suggest you voluntarily embrace it – at least for a short while.

How long is a "short while," you ask? Long enough for you to practice thinking and selling differently without broadcasting it. Seriously, if thinking and selling differently is really new for you, don't expect it to be easy, especially if you are working against a current of outdated sales philosophies. Take your time with each new element of Agility Selling. Start with one account – and don't choose the most difficult one first.

GETTING STARTED

Take a hard look at yourself. Are your four habits in place? By now, you should have a pretty good sense of that. Start addressing any imbalances. Bring all four habits into one harmonious whole; then start looking for patterns in the chaos. Take your one account and start defining their snowflake, keeping a wary eye open for any butterflies or slipping anchors. Do it again. And again. And again. Please do not try to work on the second rule of Agility Selling until you have the first one firmly established. You don't have to be perfect, but you do have to be consistent. A single event of four-habit harmony does not mean you are ready for the next step.

Once you are consistently mixing your habits and patterns, you are ready to start justifying value – for that one account. Again, you are bringing some fairly radical thinking to your business. Be patient and build a genuine success story that you can use when you are ready to come out of isolation.

Develop a deep understanding of that account's expectations and the impacts of all the possible alternatives. Start blending them to create and increase both your power and your leverage. Then experiment with your skills. Practice repositioning expectations and repositioning alternatives. Learn what works and what doesn't. Make the theory of this book fit the real world of your day-to-day selling. Then do it again. And again. And again.

By this time, you should be ready to start applying these ideas to the rest of your portfolio. Again, go slowly and deliberately. You will create the most sustainable success this way. Your sales will gradually start to grow. And grow. And grow.

After about five real successes, you are ready for the big leap out of isolation. Candidly, the first person to notice your success will likely be your manager. But don't worry. If you are experiencing success, you will have created the one thing that drives an ideal environment for change—curiosity. Your manager will likely be very curious about what you are doing differently to be doing an even better job than you were doing before. This is when you can start sharing all your chaos theory and the principles of Agility Selling. Just remember what it was like for you when you first read this stuff. It is very possible that you will need to give your manager some time to soak the concepts in. Let him or her read this book (or better yet, buy a copy as a gift). Demonstrate how Agility Selling is helping you in the simple things as well as the complex. If your manager is any good at what he or she does, the concepts of a non-linear, pattern-based approach to selling will make sense. You are on your way to even greater success.

Which brings us to two very difficult points.

What to Do If Your Manager Doesn't Get It

What if your manager doesn't get it? In fact, what if your manager hates the whole idea of non-linear, pattern-based selling? "Just follow orders," you are told. "Hit your prospecting numbers and fill in that linear report."

As painful as this situation may be, you can either go back into isolation and keep your agility to yourself or you can have a very legitimate discussion that goes something like this:

You: I can't go back to the way I used to sell.

Your manager: What do you mean?

You: I just can't do it. It doesn't work for me. But I also want to respect you and the position you are in. So I have a proposal.

Your manager: What kind of proposal? What are you talking about?

You: It's simple really. If you let me sell the way I need to sell, I will deliver the results you want. I will hit my plan and most likely exceed it. If I don't hit my numbers this quarter, I will do what you ask me to do. I will continue to play your numbers game and use my sales funnel to turn in my forecast. Deal?

You see, it's not that difficult to have this conversation. As long as you have your own four habits in place, your manager will likely give you a chance. And if your four habits are in place, you are probably making one of the safest bets you have ever made.

WHAT TO DO IF YOUR ORGANIZATION DOESN'T SUPPORT IT

Now here comes the more difficult problem. What if the organization is unable to support your agility?

Let's talk about what this really means. There will come a point at which, no matter how great you are at sales, your own company will get in the way. This can come out in a number of ways, but we are going to focus on two very specific indicators.

The first is that you have *no competitive advantage in the market.* Your organization has fallen behind in its innovation, discipline, or marketing content. Whatever you are selling is literally the same stuff your competitor has. You have no competitive edge. It doesn't matter how good you are at selling, the company doesn't have the capacity to utilize your abilities.

The second indicator is that you are *working under the wrong strategy*. Your company has put all of its resources behind a plan that is doomed to fail. You see it, your teammates see it, and perhaps even your manager sees it. This means that no matter how you try to correct the trajectory of your own strategy, your company will not be able to support what you are trying to do. It will be wasting the resources it has on other non-contributing "essentials."

In either of these situations, you have a very hard decision to make. You can either try to ride it out or leave as quickly as you can. There is no middle ground here. You are trying to fight a system, and a bad system will eventually beat a good person every time.

THE GOOD NEWS

Here is the good news. If you take the principles of Agility Selling and make them your own, you will not find yourself struggling against outdated thinking for very long. With every passing year, more and more companies are embracing the chaos. They are seeing that an agile sales force is not simply a competitive advantage; it's a full-blown business requirement. The pressure on sales executives to produce more with less has opened their eyes to new ways of thinking. And Agility Selling is one of those ways. Every company we share our philosophy with becomes excited by the possibilities agility can bring.

Compound the energy Agility Selling provides by the fact that the sales force of today is going to go through massive demographic shifts in the very near future, and you are about to see an enormous opportunity open up for talented and agile sales professionals. If you can develop a reputation for agility, you can expect to be recruited into one of the very companies that will push you toward your potential.

But don't wait for the future to come to you. Prepare in advance with your knowledge of the three chaos patterns, the four habits, the two lenses of justifying value, and the fifteen questions that enable you to keep relevant conversations at the center of your agility.

Seriously. Jump on in. The chaos in this side of the pool is just fine.

References

Battell, C. (2006). Effective listening. *Topline: How to drive sales*. Alexandria, VA: ASTD Press.

Bird, R.J. (2003). *Chaos and life: Complexity and order in evolution and thought*. New York: Columbia University Press.

Bossidy, L., & Charan, R. (2002). *The discipline of getting things done*. New York: Crown Publishing.

Briggs, J., & Peat, D. (1990). *Turbulent mirror: An illustrated guide to chaos theory and the science of wholeness*. New York: Harper Perennial.

Carnegie, D. (1926). *Public speaking: A practical course for business men*. New York: Simon & Schuster.

Carnegie, D. (1936). *How to win friends and influence people*. New York: Simon & Schuster.

Crosby, P. (1980). *Quality is free: The art of making quality certain*. New York: McGraw-Hill.

Crutchfield, J.P., Farmer, J.D., Packard, N.H., & Shaw, R.S. (1986, December). Chaos. *Scientific American, 254*(12), 46–57.

Encyclopedia of Business. (1999). Farmington Hills, MI: Thomson/Gale.

Fisher, R., & Ury, W. (1981). *Getting to yes: Negotiating agreement without giving in* (1st ed.). New York: Houghton Mifflin.

Fisher, R., Ury, W.L., & Patton, B. (1991). *Getting to yes: Negotiating agreement without giving in* (2nd ed.). New York. Penguin.

Gensler, H.J. (1996). *My formal ethics.* London: Routledge.

Gleick, J. (1987). *CHAOS: Making a new science.* New York: Penguin Books.

Goldsmith, M., & Reiter, M. (2007). *What got you here won't get you there: How successful people become even more successful.* New York: Hyperion.

Haggbloom, S.J. (2002). The 100 most eminent psychologists of the 20th century. *Review of General Psychology, 6*(2), 139–152.

H.R. Chally Corp. (2006). What makes an excellent sales force. Retrieved September 12, 2008, from www.esresearch.com/ e/home/document.php?dA=Chally_1_Comp.

Johansson, F. (2004). *The Medici effect: Breakthrough insights at the intersection of ideas, concepts, and cultures.* Boston: Harvard Business School Press.

Lambert, B. (2005, May). Forget the funnel, try alternative fuel to move sales. *Washington Business Journal.*

Lambert, B. (2009). *Ten steps to successful sales.* Alexandria, VA: ASTD Press.

Lambert, B., Ohai, T., & Kerkhoff, E. (2009). *World-class selling: New sales competencies.* Alexandria, VA: ASTD Press.

Liddell Hart, B.H. (1991). *Strategy* (2nd ed.). New York: Plume.

Lorenz, E. (1972). Does the flap of a butterfly's wings in Brazil set off a tornado in Texas? Speech presented at the 139th meeting of the American Association for the Advancement of Science.

Meginson, L.C., Mosley, D.C., & Pietrie, P.H., Jr. (1986). *Management concepts and applications* (2nd ed.). New York: Harper and Row.

Mikula, J. (2003). *Sales training.* Alexandria, VA: ASTD Press.

Miyamoto, M. (1993). Trans: T. Cleary. *The book of five rings.* Boston: Shambala.

Nickols, F. www.nickols.us/strategy_definition.htm.

Norton, D., & Kaplan, R. (2006). *Alignment.* Cambridge, MA: Harvard University Press.

Ohai, T. (2009). *Info-line: Sales coaching.* Alexandria, VA: ASTD Press.

Pelham, A. (2002, March 22). A model and initial test of the influence of firm level consulting-oriented sales force programs on sales force performance. *Journal of Personal Selling & Sales Management.*

Prochaska, J.O., & DiClemente, C.C. (1983, June). Stages and processes of self-change of smoking: Toward an integrative model of change. *Journal of Consulting Clinical Psychology,* *51*(3), 390–395.

Prochaska, J.O., DiClemente, C.C., & Norcross, J.C. (1992, September). In search of how people change: Application to addictive behaviors. *American Psychologist, 47*(9), 1102–1114.

Project Management Institute. (2010). *The project management book of knowledge (PMBOK).* Philadelphia, PA: Author.

Rackham, N. (1988). *SPIN selling.* New York: McGraw-Hill.

Rackham, N. (1989). *Major account sales strategy.* New York: McGraw-Hill.

Santucci, S. (2009, April 16). *Gaining executive-level access: Marketing strategies to help salespeople secure higher-level meetings.* Cambridge, MA: Forrester Research.

Santucci, S. (2010, February 16). *Technology buyer insight study: Preferred or exclusive vendor relationships. As buyers stratify their suppliers, sales must re-evaluate how to deliver value.* Cambridge, MA: Forrester Research.

Santucci, S. (2010, February 17). *Technology buyer insight study: The expanding role of procurement in the buying process.* Cambridge, MA: Forrester Research.

Santucci, S. (2010, February 18). *Technology buyer insight study: Executive involvement in the buying process.*

Changing buying patterns create opportunities for vendors. Cambridge, MA: Forrester Research.

Santucci, S. (2010, April 19). *Technology buyer insight study: Are salespeople prepared for executive conversations?* Cambridge, MA: Forrester Research.

Steil, L.K., & Bommelje, R.K. (2004). *Listening leaders: The ten golden rules to listen, lead, and succeed.* Edina, MN: Beaver's Pond Press.

Stevens, H., & Kinni, T. (2007). *Achieve sales excellence: The 7 customer rules for becoming the new sales professional.* Avon, MA: Platinum Press.

Strogatz, S. (2003). *Sync: The emerging science of spontaneous order.* New York: Hyperion.

Wheatley, M.J. (1994). *Leadership and the new science.* San Francisco: Berrett-Koehler.

About the Authors

Tim Ohai, M.S., is the founder and president of Growth & Associates, a consulting group that focuses on solving sales and marketing problems. With well over a decade's worth of experience in developing sales team performance, he consistently helps Fortune 500 companies design and implement selling solutions internationally, build sales systems that increase revenue and customer loyalty, and create genuine coaching cultures. He is often asked to consult larger, more complex issues, especially around the topics of redesigning sales organizations and leading organizational change. His expertise and enthusiasm have taken him to Latin America, Europe, Africa, Asia, and the Middle East as both consultant and keynote speaker. He has a master's of science in industrial/organizational psychology, but don't hold that against him.

You can reach Tim via e-mail at Tim@SalesChaos.com or online at www.saleschaos.com/about_Tim.

Brian Lambert, Ph.D., is a senior analyst with Forrester Research, serving technology sales enablement professionals. In this role, he covers the strategy, technology, and execution associated with helping sales team members achieve business outcomes through the alignment of cross-functional resources in sales, marketing, and portfolio teams. He also researches the key functions associated with sales enablement, including sales models, sales structure and alignment, sales messaging, content, knowledge management, sales talent management, sales training, sales readiness, and metrics. Brian has fifteen years of experience in all facets of sales, sales management, and sales training and is an internationally recognized expert on transforming sales team systems, processes, and people. He has a master's of science in human resource and information resource management and a Ph.D. in organization and management, and you may hold that against him.

You may reach Brian via e-mail at Brian@SalesChaos.com or online at www.saleschaos.com/about_Brian.

Index

A

Accountability, 197–198

Achieving results through others, 118. *See also* influence

Agile sales conversations, 244–246. *See also* sales conversations

Agility, 55–56; defined, 89; navigating chaos with, 169–175

Agility Selling, 94, 107–108; defining, 101–102; history of, 100; pattern recognition, 97–99; and patterns, 95; review, 169–175, 231–235; rules of, 102–103, 170, 264–265. *See also* Four Habits of Agile Sellers

Alignment (Norton and Kaplan), 164

Alternatives to expectations, 185–186; best alternative to a negotiated agreement (BATNA), 208; blending expectations and alternatives, 221–229, 235; introduction to, 207; Lens of Alternatives, 193, 208; negotiation, 208–209; shifting alternatives, 218–219; six buyers' alternatives, 209–212, 233–234; three sellers' alternatives, 212–213, 234; unexpected alternatives, 215–218; using alternatives, 213–215. *See also* expectations

Anchor points, 41–42, 58–59, 95; and continuous improvement, 56–57; and execution, 151; impact of, 46; introduction to, 44–45; making agile adjustments, 55–56; non-linear reality of business, 54–55; order of, 52–54; pattern density, 43; power of non-linear forces, 42–43; review, 82; sales fundamentals, 46–47; sales processes, 47–49; sales relationships, 49–50; sales